GCSE English Literature AQA Anthology

Relationships

The Study Guide
Higher Level

This book is a step-by-step guide to becoming an expert on the Anthology part of your GCSE English Literature exam.

It's got everything you need to know — annotated poems, key themes, exam advice and worked essays.

It's ideal for use as a classroom study book or a revision guide.

What CGP is all about

Our sole aim here at CGP is to produce the highest quality books — carefully written, immaculately presented and dangerously close to being funny.

Then we work our socks off to get them out to you — at the cheapest possible prices.

CONTENTS

Section Four — Poetry Techniques

Section Five — The Poetry Exam

Section Six — Controlled Assessment

Section Seven — How to Write an A* Answer

Published by CGP

Editors:
Luke von Kotze, Edward Robinson, Hayley Thompson, Karen Wells
Produced with:
Alison Smith, Peter Thomas, Nicola Woodfin
Contributors:
Caroline Bagshaw

With thanks to Katherine Reed and Linda Robinson for the proofreading
and Jan Greenway for copyright research.

ISBN: 978 1 84762 488 8

Groovy website: www.cgpbooks.co.uk
Jolly bits of clipart from CorelDRAW®
Printed by Elanders Ltd, Newcastle upon Tyne.

Based on the classic CGP style created by Richard Parsons.

How to Use this Book

This guide is for anyone studying the <u>Relationships</u> cluster of the AQA GCSE English Literature <u>Poetry Anthology</u>. You'll have to either answer an <u>exam question</u> on the poems, or write about them for your <u>controlled assessment</u> — your teacher will tell you which.

Sections One and Two are About The Poems

There are usually <u>two pages</u> about <u>each poem</u>. This is what the pages look like:

There's a nice picture of <u>the poet</u> and some info about their life.

Important or tricky bits of the poem are <u>highlighted</u> and <u>explained</u>.

Difficult words are defined in the <u>poem dictionary</u>.

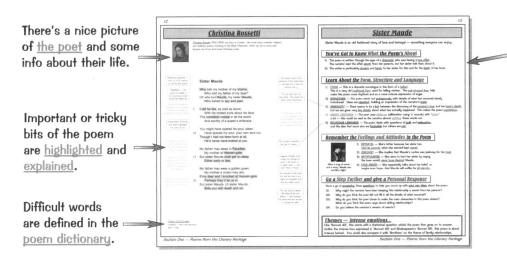

On the right-hand page there are <u>notes</u> about the poem. They include:

- <u>what happens</u> in the poem
- the <u>form</u>, <u>structure</u> and <u>language</u> the poet uses
- the <u>feelings</u> and <u>attitudes</u> in the poem
- a few questions asking you about <u>your feelings</u> on the poem.

If the poem's a bit of a <u>long one</u>, it'll be spread over <u>two pages</u>. One of these will be a <u>pull-out flap</u>. Don't panic. There are full instructions on what to do:

THIS IS A FLAP.
FOLD THIS PAGE OUT.

It's Really Important You Know Your Stuff

Whether you're doing the exam or the controlled assessment, you need to be really <u>familiar</u> with the poems.

1) You <u>won't notice</u> everything about a poem on <u>first reading</u>. Keep reading these poems over and over and <u>over again</u>.

2) If you notice something about a poem then <u>jot it down</u> — there's <u>no limit</u> to the number of <u>valid points</u> that could be made about these poems.

3) Make sure you have a go at <u>answering</u> those questions at the bottom of the right-hand page.

The questions are designed to make you <u>think for yourself</u> about the poems. You'll get <u>marks</u> in both the exam and the controlled assessment for giving <u>your own ideas</u> and <u>opinions</u> on the texts — it's called a <u>personal response</u>.

Nigel's first response to the poems wasn't all that positive.

How to Use this Book

You've got to make <u>comparisons</u> between the poems in your writing — so I've included two dead handy sections showing their <u>similarities</u> and <u>differences</u>. No need to thank me.

Section Three is About Themes and Ideas

This section will help you make <u>links</u> between the <u>themes</u> presented in the poems — it'll give you loads of <u>ideas</u> of what to write about in your exam or controlled assessment.

A <u>different theme</u> is looked at on <u>each page</u>.

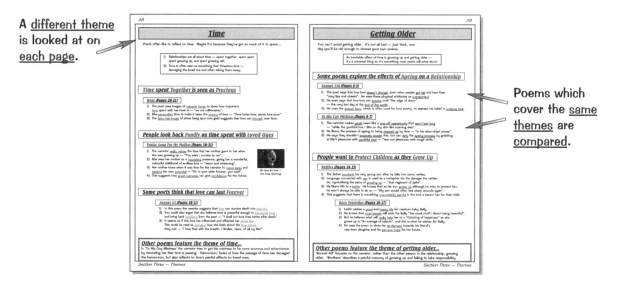

Poems which cover the <u>same</u> themes are <u>compared</u>.

Section Four is About Poetry Techniques

1) This section is all about <u>form</u>, structure and <u>language</u>.

2) It looks at how different poets use features like <u>rhyme</u>, <u>rhythm</u> and <u>imagery</u> to create <u>effects</u> — it's something the examiners are <u>dead keen</u> for you to <u>understand</u> and <u>write about</u>.

Each term is <u>explained</u>...

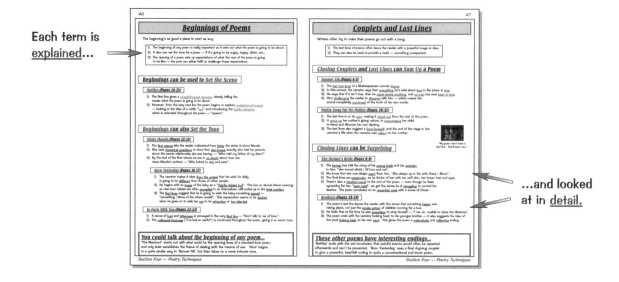

...and looked at in <u>detail</u>.

How to Use this Book

If you're studying these poems for the <u>Unit 2 exam</u>, then you need <u>Section Five</u>.
If you're doing these poems for your <u>Unit 5 controlled assessment</u>, look at <u>Section Six</u>.

Section *Five* Tells You What to Do in Your Exam

This is where you can find out <u>exactly</u> what's involved in your <u>Unit 2: Poetry Across Time</u> exam.

There are <u>questions</u> like the ones you'll get in the exam...

... and <u>sample plans</u> to show you different ways to plan your essay.

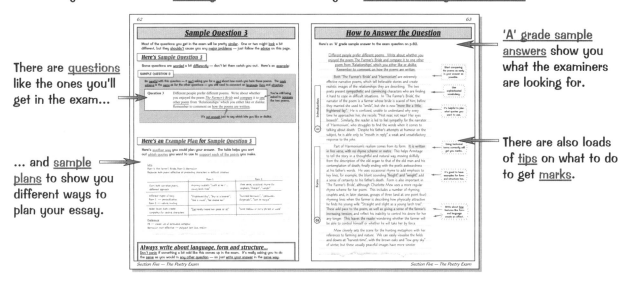

'A' grade sample <u>answers</u> show you what the examiners are looking for.

There are also loads of <u>tips</u> on what to do to get <u>marks</u>.

Section *Six* Tells You What to Do in Your Controlled Assessment

This section gives you the lowdown on the <u>Unit 5: Exploring Poetry</u> controlled assessment.

There are some <u>example questions</u> like the ones you'll be given, as well as...

...tips on <u>planning</u> and <u>preparing</u> for your assessment piece...

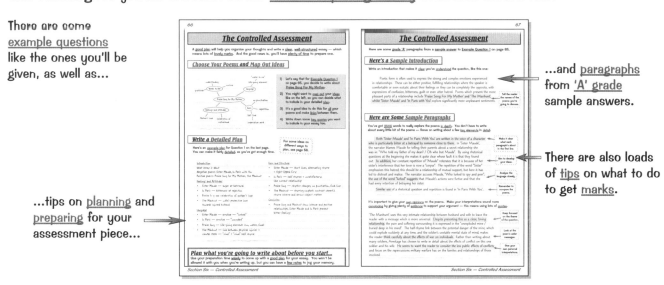

...and <u>paragraphs</u> from <u>'A' grade</u> sample answers.

There are also loads of <u>tips</u> on what to do to get <u>marks</u>.

Section *Seven* Tells You How to Write An A* Answer

1) Whether you're aiming for an A* or not, this is a really <u>useful</u> section — there are <u>tons of tips</u> for how to <u>improve</u> your work.

2) It tells you how to get the <u>highest marks</u> and gives you <u>loads of examples</u> showing how to do it.

William Shakespeare

William Shakespeare (1564-1616) was a successful playwright and poet. He was born in Stratford-upon-Avon, Warwickshire, but lived in London for most of his life. This sonnet is the 116th in a series of 154 on the theme of love.

Sonnet 116

He believes that nothing can stop true love from lasting.

Impediments is a word used in traditional marriage services — it reminds us of weddings.

This metaphor compares love to the Pole Star which stays in the same place in the sky and helps sailors to navigate.

It's within Time's power to take away youth and beauty.

The poet guarantees us that what he is saying is true.

Let me not to the marriage of true minds
Admit impediments; love is not love
Which alters when it alteration finds,
Or bends with the remover to remove.
5 O no it is an ever-fixed mark,
That looks on tempests and is never shaken;
It is the star to every wand'ring bark,
Whose worth's unknown, although his height be taken.
Love's not Time's fool, though rosy lips and cheeks
10 Within his bending sickle's compass come;
Love alters not with his brief hours and weeks,
But bears it out even to the edge of doom.
   If this be error and upon me proved,
   I never writ, nor no man ever loved.

True love does not change when faced with difficult or unexpected circumstances.

Near repetition suggests that love is constant — it won't change the way appearances do.

The star's height can be mathematically measured, but its value to the ships it guides is immeasurable.

Time is personified, which makes the battle between time and love dramatic.

Any measure of time is short for love, because love lasts till the end of time.

POEM DICTIONARY
impediment — something that stops something or holds it up
bark — small ship with sails
sickle — a sharp, curved tool for cutting corn always used on pictures of Old Father Time and Death
compass — reach
doom — doomsday: the very last day at the end of the world

Sonnet 116

Shakespeare argues that no matter what happens, true love won't change. Isn't that nice.

You've Got to Know What the Poem's About

1) Shakespeare is writing about how constant true love is. It can't be shaken, even when people change as they get older — if their love is real love then it stays just as powerful as ever.

2) If it really is genuine love, then it doesn't change when circumstances change.

3) He says that if what he says isn't true, then he never wrote anything and no man has ever been in love. Since we know he did write, and men do love he's saying his words on love are true.

Learn About the Form, Structure and Language

1) FORM — This poem is a sonnet. Sonnets were a popular form of poetry in Shakespeare's day and they were often used for writing about love. This sonnet is made up of three quatrains with a rhyming couplet at the end. The regular rhyme scheme gives the poem a sense of order and completeness.

2) STRUCTURE — The quatrains all discuss the same idea of love being unchanging in slightly different ways and using different imagery. The final couplet is the narrator's guarantee that he's telling the truth.

3) LANGUAGE ABOUT SAILING — True love is shown to be reliable — it guides us in an uncertain and stormy world.

4) LANGUAGE ABOUT TIME AND AGEING — When we get older we look different, perhaps not as attractive, but true love isn't tricked by the effects of Time — it remains the same. Love isn't at the mercy of time — it has no end.

Look at the glossary on pages 72 and 73 for definitions of words like 'sonnet' and 'quatrain'.

Remember the Feelings and Attitudes in the Poem

"It's all done with satellites now."

1) DEVOTION — The voice in the poem is declaring a love which will not change.

2) CONSTANCY — He sees love as fixed and eternal — something which won't change even when the object of his love changes.

3) TRUE LOVE — It's not a shallow, superficial love which is based on what the loved one looks like.

Go a Step Further and give a Personal Response

Have a go at answering these questions to help you come up with your own ideas about the poem:

Q1. Do you think Shakespeare is writing about the love of younger or older people? Why?

Q2. Can you give this poem a title which you think sums up the ideas in it?

Q3. What effect does the personification of time have on your reading of the poem?

Q4. To what extent would you say that this was a poem about love in general, rather than a love poem to someone in particular?

Themes — attitudes towards love...

Like 'Sonnet 43', this poem deals with an ideal version of what love should be like. You could also compare it with 'To His Coy Mistress', which also deals with the idea of the effects of ageing on love, although it does it from a very different angle.

Andrew Marvell

Contrasts vastness and nothingness of death with how brief but full of possibilities life is.

He tells her she'll die and be buried a virgin to be eaten by worms. He's trying to shock her into giving him what he wants.

Repetition of "Now" makes it sound like a call to action.

Violent language and imagery suggest he may be getting impatient with her.

But at my back I always hear
Time's wingèd chariot hurrying near;
And yonder all before us lie
Deserts of vast eternity.
25 Thy beauty shall no more be found,
Nor, in thy marble vault, shall sound
My echoing song; then worms shall try
That long preserved virginity,
And your quaint honour turn to dust,
30 And into ashes all my lust.
The grave's a fine and private place,
But none, I think, do there embrace.

Now therefore, while the youthful hue
Sits on thy skin like morning dew,
35 And while thy willing soul transpires
At every pore with instant fires,
Now let us sport us while we may,
And now, like amorous birds of prey,
Rather at once our time devour
40 Than languish in his slow-chapt power.
Let us roll all our strength and all
Our sweetness up into one ball,
And tear our pleasures with rough strife
Through the iron gates of life.
45 Thus, though we cannot make our sun
Stand still, yet we will make him run.

Metaphor from Greek mythology — Helios the Sun god rides his chariot across the sky. Shows the passing of time.

He's being sarcastic.

"There'll be nobody to hug you in your grave."

He takes it for granted she's willing — you could read this as ignoring what she wants, or trying to convince her it's what she wants.

Passionate language.

This simile draws attention to the power and passion of these creatures to emphasise his desire for immediate satisfaction.

Wants them to be united.

Defiantly standing up to time — time will have to run to keep up with them.

POEM DICTIONARY
coy — shy
mistress — a man's long term companion/sweetheart
quaint — too prim and proper or old-fashioned
slow-chapt — slow jawed, i.e. chewing slowly

Andrew Marvell

Andrew Marvell (1621-1678) was born in Yorkshire and raised in Hull. After studying at Cambridge, he travelled in Europe, before taking a post as a tutor. He's known as a metaphysical poet, as he wrote about philosophical subjects like life and soul.

To His Coy Mistress

"If only we had unlimited time then your shyness wouldn't be a problem."

A river in the North of England — Marvell's local river. Not particularly romantic.

Overstates his love to the point of being comic.

He exaggerates the time he would spend on flattery if there were no limits.

Large river in India, worshipped as a goddess.

Reference to the Old Testament exaggerates the time scale, emphasising his sarcasm.

Something that will never happen or that some believe will happen at the end of the world.

He focuses on her physical attributes.

He tells her she's worth spending all this time on and he does want to be able to love her in this way.

Had we but world enough, and time,
This coyness, Lady, were no crime,
We would sit down and think which way
To walk and pass our long love's day.
5   Thou by the Indian Ganges' side
Shouldst rubies find; I by the tide
Of Humber would complain. I would
Love you ten years before the Flood,
And you should, if you please, refuse
10   Till the conversion of the Jews.
My vegetable love should grow
Vaster than empires, and more slow;
An hundred years should go to praise
Thine eyes, and on thy forehead gaze;
15   Two hundred to adore each breast;
But thirty thousand to the rest;
An age at least to every part,
And the last age should show your heart.
For, Lady, you deserve this state,
20   Nor would I love at lower rate.

THIS IS A FLAP.
FOLD THIS PAGE OUT.

To His Coy Mistress

In this poem the narrator is trying to get his mistress to go to bed with him — how romantic.

You've Got to Know What the Poem's About

1) The narrator is telling the woman he loves that she shouldn't play <u>hard to get</u> and want to be wooed and flattered and given presents — there <u>isn't time</u>.

2) He says they should <u>enjoy</u> each other whilst they are <u>young</u> and <u>attractive</u>. He tries lots of different arguments to <u>persuade</u> her.

Learn About the Form, Structure and Language

1) <u>FORM</u> — This poem has a first person narrator — this makes it clear that this is a <u>direct appeal</u> to the coy mistress of the title. It's made up of <u>rhyming couplets</u> which make the poem sound <u>witty</u> and <u>well constructed</u>.

2) <u>STRUCTURE</u> — The first stanza explains that he would <u>wish</u> to <u>spend forever</u> wooing her, the second that he <u>can't</u> because they <u>won't live forever</u>, the third stanza suggests they should <u>grab</u> their pleasures <u>while they can</u>. This follows a traditional structure for <u>arguments</u> — if A, but B, therefore C.

3) <u>HYPERBOLE</u> — He mocks his mistress's <u>romantic ideas</u> of love. His sense of <u>frustration</u> is beginning to show through his <u>irony</u> and <u>exaggeration</u>.

4) <u>LANGUAGE ABOUT DEATH</u> — He reminds his mistress that <u>time is passing</u>. He moves his <u>argument</u> on, saying that <u>one day</u> they will <u>both be dead</u>.

5) <u>AGGRESSIVE LANGUAGE</u> — As the poem goes on he becomes <u>more direct</u> in expressing his <u>desire</u> for her. He uses <u>passionate</u> and <u>violent imagery</u>.

Remember the Feelings and Attitudes in the Poem

Sorry love — you're just not my type.

1) <u>IMPATIENCE</u> — He doesn't want to have a <u>long courtship</u> of her.

2) <u>URGENCY</u> — Time is <u>moving on</u> and he feels that they need to enjoy being together now.

3) <u>RELUCTANCE</u> — From the <u>increasing frustration</u> he shows, it appears that she's <u>unwilling</u> to have sex with him.

Go a Step Further and give a Personal Response

Have a go at <u>answering</u> these <u>questions</u> to help you come up with <u>your own ideas</u> about the poem:

Q1. How much do we find out about the mistress and her thoughts and feelings?

Q2. What impression does the phrase "vegetable love" give about his feelings?

Q3. Is there any evidence in the poem that his mistress is really modest, or is she just playing hard to get?

Q4. Some people argue that the narrator of the poem is losing his temper, others that he is making a well-ordered argument. What do you think?

Themes — the passage of time and how it affects people...

The effects of time and death are also discussed in 'Sonnet 116' and 'Sonnet 43'.
The role of physical passion is also a theme in 'Hour' and 'In Paris With You'.

Charlotte Mew

She's a fairly good housewife — she does what is expected of her in the relationship apart from loving her husband.

She is near silent and only speaks to animals. She sounds withdrawn and depressed.

Could suggest a link back to the imagery of the hunt.

Carries connotations both of an unspoilt freedom and of a rejection of people.

Symbolising his sinking hope that she will ever come to him freely.

Sounds sympathetic and also suggests that she remains a virgin and unchanged from when they first married.

Describes her as animal-like — the source of both his desire and frustration.

20 She does the work about the house
As well as most, but like a mouse:
    Happy enough to chat and play
    With birds and rabbits and such as they,
    So long as men-folk keep away.
25 'Not near, not near!' her eyes beseech
When one of us comes within reach.
    The women say that beasts in stall
    Look round like children at her call.
    I've hardly heard her speak at all.

30 Shy as a leveret, swift as he,
Straight and slight as a young larch tree,
Sweet as the first wild violets, she,
To her wild self. But what to me?

The short days shorten and the oaks are brown,
35   The blue smoke rises to the low grey sky,
One leaf in the still air falls slowly down,
    A magpie's spotted feathers lie
On the black earth spread white with rime,
The berries redden up to Christmas-time.
40   What's Christmas-time without there be
    Some other in the house than we!

    She sleeps up in the attic there
    Alone, poor maid. 'Tis but a stair
Betwixt us. Oh! my God! the down,
45 The soft young down of her; the brown,
The brown of her – her eyes, her hair, her hair!

Animal imagery — she is linked with small prey animals.

We hear her thoughts pleading for men to keep away from her.

The farm animals trust her — maybe suggests he's jealous of them.

Short stanza. Sibilance emphasises her link with nature.

Rhetorical question — breaks his happier thoughts of her in springtime imagery and takes him back to the winter scene.

Winter is used to suggest the decay and death of his hopes.

Christmas is about the birth of a child — they have no children because of her refusal of him.

He is aware of her physical presence, adding to his frustration.

He's breaking down — losing control.

POEM DICTIONARY
bide — wait
fay — a fairy
leveret — a young hare
rime — ice

Charlotte Mew

Charlotte Mew (1869-1928) was born in London. Despite attracting praise for her poetry from Thomas Hardy, Virginia Woolf and Siegfried Sassoon, Mew never achieved commercial success and spent most of her life in poverty.

May suggest she didn't have much choice in the matter.

The Farmer's Bride

He was too busy farming to have time to court her properly.

She wasn't afraid until after they were married.

Simile to show how sudden this change was — winter days go dark very quickly.

Three Summers since I chose a maid,
Too young maybe – but more's to do
At harvest-time than bide and woo.
    When us was wed she turned afraid
5 Of love and me and all things human;
Like the shut of a winter's day
Her smile went out, and 'twasn't a woman –
    More like a little frightened fay.
        One night, in the Fall, she runned away.

She's not just afraid of him, but of everyone.

10 'Out 'mong the sheep, her be,' they said,
Should properly have been abed;
But sure enough she wasn't there
Lying awake with her wide brown stare.
    So over seven-acre field and up-along across the down
15 We chased her, flying like a hare
    Before our lanterns. To Church-Town
All in a shiver and a scare
We caught her, fetched her home at last
    And turned the key upon her, fast.

She seems to be frightened of falling asleep.

Hunting imagery — suggests her terror.

Her fear is expressed physically — perhaps like an animal.

The whole village seems to be involved — this adds to the sense that she's being hunted, but also suggests that everyone thinks her behaviour's abnormal.

Dialect of the farmer — we can hear his voice, and it's one he shares with his community.

Mention of the church — perhaps a reference to the fact that they are officially married.

Rather sinister — she's been locked up securely.

The Farmer's Bride

This poem tells the unhappy story of a farmer and his wife. It's filled with rural imagery — setting the scene and providing a source for similes and metaphors.

You've Got to Know What the Poem's About

1) A farmer has been married for three years but his bride is frightened of men.

2) In the poem he thinks about this, telling the story of how the relationship went wrong. He doesn't blame himself. He desires his wife.

3) Her rejection of him is almost unbearable for him but he expresses his thoughts in a fairly matter-of-fact way. By the end it seems he may be struggling to resist taking her by force.

Learn About the Form, Structure and Language

1) FORM — The poem is a dramatic monologue, mostly in iambic tetrameter with a rhyme scheme that varies through the poem. This helps give the poem a strong rhythm driving the narrative forward without becoming predictable.

2) STRUCTURE — The farmer tells the story of the marriage through the first two stanzas, then goes on to discuss how his wife is now, how he feels towards her, his sadness and his desire.

3) LANGUAGE ABOUT NATURE — The farmer uses imagery mainly taken from the natural world. This both reflects on who the farmer is, and in his descriptions of his wife links her to images of nature and wildness. In the second stanza she is likened to a hunted hare.

4) DIALECT — The poem contains many dialect words which help to give a strong sense of the farmer's character. We can hear his voice in his language and in his grammar — this adds to the drama as it helps us picture the people involved.

Remember the Feelings and Attitudes in the Poem

"Maybe you should just talk to the guy — tell him how you feel."

1) FRUSTRATION — He wants to have a sexual relationship with her and to have children but she's unwilling.

2) DESIRE — The farmer is clearly attracted to his wife. This is expressed both in the imagery he uses to describe her and the way he breaks down at the end of the poem.

3) FEAR — There is a sense of foreboding — the farmer is struggling to keep his desire for her under control and there is little to suggest that there will be a happy ending for the married couple.

Go a Step Further and give a Personal Response

Have a go at answering these questions to help you come up with your own ideas about the poem:

Q1.   How far do you blame the farmer for his wife's attitude?

Q2.   To what extent would you describe 'The Farmer's Bride' as a love poem?

Q3.   How does the poet use the different seasons to describe the relationship?

Q4.   Can you write an ending to this story? What happens next?

Themes — unhappy love...

You could compare this poem with either 'Hour' or 'In Paris With You' which give more modern accounts of how love can be an intense experience. Both this poem and 'To His Coy Mistress' have a frustrated narrator, but this is more tragic whereas the other's more witty and comic.

Elizabeth Barrett Browning

Elizabeth Barrett Browning (1806-1861) was born into an affluent family in County Durham. A successful poet in her own right, she was influenced heavily by (and had a profound influence on) the poetry of her husband, Robert Browning.

Sonnet 43

Repetition throughout poem emphasises the depth of her love.

Direct address makes this seem more personal.

How do I love thee? Let me count the ways! —
I love thee to the depth and breadth and height
My soul can reach, when feeling out of sight
For the ends of Being and Ideal Grace.

Religious ideas and imagery — suggests a sense of awe when she thinks about her love.

She loves without expectation of reward.

5   I love thee to the level of everyday's
Most quiet need, by sun and candlelight —
I love thee freely, as men strive for Right, —
I love thee purely, as they turn from Praise;

Each repetition of the phrase is followed by a different idea — showing how her love has many aspects and is all-encompassing.

I love thee with the passion, put to use
10   In my old griefs, ... and with my childhood's faith:
I love thee with the love I seemed to lose

She links her love to ideals of virtuous conduct — she thinks her love is morally right and pure.

She loves him with the passion and intense emotion that religion gave her as a child.

With my lost Saints, — I love thee with the breath,
Smiles, tears, of all my life! — and, if God choose,
I shall but love thee better after death.

Links her love to the idea of heaven — suggests its purity and spiritual nature.

Her love covers her whole life — it isn't just about the good times.

Section One — Poems from the Literary Heritage

Sonnet 43

This poem mixes a declaration of love up with a lot of religious imagery — it's a heady brew.
It's from a sequence of sonnets written for Robert Browning, called "Sonnets from the Portuguese".

You've Got to Know What the Poem's About

1) This is a <u>love poem</u>, where Barrett Browning expresses her intense love for her husband-to-be, <u>Robert Browning</u>.

2) She loves him so <u>deeply</u> that she sees their love as <u>spiritual</u> and <u>sacred</u>. She counts all of the <u>different ways</u> in which she loves him.

3) Her love is so <u>great</u> that she believes she will love him even <u>after death</u>.

Learn About the Form, Structure and Language

1) <u>FORM</u> — Sonnet form is traditionally used for love poetry. This is in <u>Petrarchan</u> form, with eight lines (an <u>octave</u>) followed by six lines (a <u>sestet</u>).

2) <u>STRUCTURE</u> — The octave presents the <u>theme</u> of the poem — here it's comparing the poet's <u>love</u> and <u>religious ideas</u>. The sestet develops this theme by making comparisons between the <u>intensity</u> of her feelings for her lover and the kinds of love she felt as a <u>child</u>. As the sestet develops it shows she loves him with the <u>emotions</u> of an <u>entire life</u> — from <u>childhood</u>, through the <u>loss of innocence</u> (perhaps adolescence?) through to, and past, <u>death</u>.

3) <u>REPETITION</u> — Using the same words repeatedly at the start of phrases is called <u>anaphora</u>. This is a rhetorical device that is used in the <u>Bible</u>. It makes her poem seem like a <u>prayer</u>.

4) <u>RELIGIOUS LANGUAGE</u> — Her love seems like a <u>religion</u> to her in the way that it touches <u>all aspects</u> of her life and gives meaning to her existence. Her love is <u>unconditional</u> like the ideal of religious faith.

Remember the Feelings and Attitudes in the Poem

Sonnet 44 — "I love thee
more than doughnuts..."

1) <u>DEEP AND LASTING LOVE</u> — The poet uses the <u>strength</u> of <u>spiritual love</u> to emphasise how <u>strongly</u> she feels about her <u>husband</u>.

2) <u>UNSELFISH LOVE</u> — She asks for <u>nothing in return</u>.

3) <u>VIRTUE</u> — The poem makes her love seem <u>morally</u> and <u>spiritually right</u>.

Go a Step Further and give a Personal Response

Have a go at <u>answering</u> these <u>questions</u> to help you come up with <u>your own ideas</u> about the poem:

Q1. What title might you give this sonnet?

Q2. How realistic do you think this expression of love is?

Q3. How does the poet use religious themes to symbolise the relationship?

Q4. How would you describe the character of the narrator?

Themes — love after death...

This poem holds out the possibility of such an intense love that it lasts beyond the grave, which is the exact opposite message to that of 'To His Coy Mistress'. 'Sonnet 43' also picks out different aspects of her love in a way that you could compare with 'Ghazal'.

Christina Rossetti

Christina Rossetti (1830-1894) was born in London. She wrote many romantic, religious and children's poems, including 'In the Bleak Midwinter', which was set to music and became one of our best-loved Christmas carols.

Sister Maude

> Who told my mother of my shame,
>   Who told my father of my dear?
> Oh who but Maude, my sister Maude,
>   Who lurked to spy and peer.
>
> 5 Cold he lies, as cold as stone,
>   With his clotted curls about his face:
> The comeliest corpse in all the world
>   And worthy of a queen's embrace.
>
> You might have spared his soul, sister,
> 10   Have spared my soul, your own soul too:
> Though I had not been born at all,
>   He'd never have looked at you.
>
> My father may sleep in Paradise,
>   My mother at Heaven-gate:
> 15 But sister Maude shall get no sleep
>   Either early or late.
>
> My father may wear a golden gown,
>   My mother a crown may win;
> If my dear and I knocked at Heaven-gate
> 20   Perhaps they'd let us in:
> But sister Maude, oh sister Maude,
>   Bide *you* with death and sin.

Annotations (left side):

Rhetorical questions — draw us in by making us wait for the answer.

Repetition — she wants the reader to be absolutely certain where the blame lies.

This emotive, negative language turns us against Maude and makes us sympathetic with the narrator.

Juxtaposition of beauty and death highlights her sense of loss.

Spiteful comment — and establishes that Maude did what she did out of jealousy.

Repetition of "sister" emphasises the closeness of their relationship and so the seriousness of the betrayal.

Alliteration helps link sister Maude with sin — as with spy in the first stanza.

Annotations (right side):

She doesn't seem to be ashamed of the relationship — perhaps this is how her parents view it.

It's not clear how her lover died. This makes the poem seem mysterious.

The alliteration of hard 'c' sounds emphasises the strong rhythm — which makes the poem sound more energetic and angry.

The narrator's parents may get to heaven.

Suggests Maude won't escape her feelings of guilt in life (early) or in death (late) — she won't 'Rest in Peace'.

The narrator thinks that her and her lover's sins might be forgivable, but that her sister's aren't.

The last stanza repeats the ideas of the one before — this increases the sense that the narrator is cursing her sister.

POEM DICTIONARY
comeliest — the most attractive
bide — stay

Sister Maude

Sister Maude is an old fashioned story of love and betrayal — something everyone can enjoy.

You've Got to Know What the Poem's About

1) The poem is written through the eyes of a <u>character</u> who was having a <u>love affair</u>.
The narrator kept the affair <u>secret</u> from her parents, but her sister told them about it.

2) The writer is particularly <u>abusive</u> and <u>harsh</u> to her sister for this and for the <u>death</u> of her lover.

Learn About the Form, Structure and Language

1) <u>FORM</u> — This is a dramatic monologue in the form of a <u>ballad</u>.
This is a very old <u>traditional form</u> used for telling stories. The <u>end-stopped lines</u> help make this poem more rhythmic and so a more intense expression of anger.

2) <u>STRUCTURE</u> — The poem starts out <u>ambiguously</u> with details of what has occurred slowly introduced. Ideas are <u>repeated</u>, building an impression of the narrator's <u>anger</u>.

3) <u>AMBIGUITY</u> — There seems to be a <u>link</u> between the discovery of the <u>narrator's love</u> and her <u>lover's death</u>, but we are given very <u>few details</u> about what has actually happened. This makes the poem <u>mysterious</u>.

4) <u>ANGRY LANGUAGE</u> — The poet uses <u>sibilance</u> (alliteration using 's' sounds) with "<u>sister</u>" a lot — this could be read as the narrator almost <u>spitting</u> these words out.

5) <u>RELIGIOUS LANGUAGE</u> — The poem deals with questions of <u>guilt</u> and <u>redemption</u>, and the idea that some sins are <u>forgivable</u> but others are <u>not</u>.

Remember the Feelings and Attitudes in the Poem

After a mug of cocoa and a story, Maude was out like a light.

1) <u>BETRAYAL</u> — She's bitter because her sister has <u>told her parents</u> what she wanted kept <u>secret</u>.

2) <u>JEALOUSY</u> — She implies that Maude's motive was jealousy for her <u>lover</u>.

3) <u>SPITEFULNESS</u> — She aims to hurt her sister by saying the lover would <u>never have desired</u> Maude.

4) <u>COLD ANGER</u> — She repeatedly talks about her belief, or maybe even hope, that Maude will suffer for <u>all eternity</u>.

Go a Step Further and give a Personal Response

Have a go at <u>answering</u> these <u>questions</u> to help you come up with <u>your own ideas</u> about the poem:

Q1.   Why might the narrator have been keeping this relationship a secret from her parents?

Q2.   Why do you think the poet did not fill in all the details of what occurred?

Q3.   Why do you think the poet chose to make the main characters in this poem sisters?
What do you think this poem says about sibling relationships?

Q4.   Do you believe the narrator's version of events?

Themes — intense emotions...

Like 'Sonnet 43', this starts with a rhetorical question which the poem then goes on to answer.
Unlike the intense love expressed in 'Sonnet 43' and Shakespeare's 'Sonnet 116', this poem is about intense hatred. You could also compare it with 'Brothers' on the theme of family relationships.

Vernon Scannell

Vernon Scannell (1922-2007) was born in Lincolnshire but moved frequently during his childhood. After a stint in the army, he became a professional boxer and then an English teacher. Many of his poems were shaped by his wartime experience.

Nettles

My son aged three fell in the nettle bed.
'Bed' seemed a curious name for those green spears,
That regiment of spite behind the shed:
It was no place for rest. With sobs and tears
5   The boy came seeking comfort and I saw
White blisters beaded on his tender skin.
We soothed him till his pain was not so raw.
At last he offered us a watery grin,
And then I took my hook and honed the blade
10   And went outside and slashed in fury with it
Till not a nettle in that fierce parade
Stood upright any more. Next task: I lit
A funeral pyre to burn the fallen dead.
But in two weeks the busy sun and rain
15   Had called up tall recruits behind the shed:
My son would often feel sharp wounds again.

The first line is a matter-of-fact description of the main event of the poem — makes it seem everyday and real.

A weapon with a sharp point as well as the stalk of a plant.

The poem focuses in on the boy's pain and his physical vulnerability.

He can't take away the pain entirely.

The nettles are like soldiers killed in battle.

This seems to suggest not only physical wounds but the emotional pain we all go through in life.

Suggests comfort and safety — so he sees this as an ironic term.

Personification of the nettles — makes them sound like an army, and suggests they attacked the boy on purpose.

Juxtaposition of his careful preparation and his furious attacks — emphasises the sharp contrast in his reactions.

Being "called up" is being ordered to join the army — suggests they'll never be defeated as there will always be more nettles.

POEM DICTIONARY
honed — sharpened

Nettles

This poem starts out being a fairly straightforward anecdote about parental love — but by the end the poet makes clear that he's actually writing about something a bit broader than that.

You've Got to Know What the Poem's About

1) A three-year-old boy falls into a bed of nettles and is badly stung.
2) His father comforts him, then goes out and cuts down and burns the nettles.
3) Two weeks later they have grown back. This simple event is used to explore suffering and the powerlessness of parents to stop their children from getting hurt in life.
4) The physical pain of the nettles has a deeper meaning of the emotional suffering which the father knows his son will have to experience in life. His inability to destroy the nettles is a metaphor for the fact that the father can't protect his son from the pains of living.

Learn About the Form, Structure and Language

1) FORM — This is a narrative poem with a first person narrator — this emphasises that the poem is talking about personal experiences. Use of enjambment makes it sound more like a story being told to the reader.
2) STRUCTURE — The poem goes through the story in a straightforward way, introducing events in the order they happened.
3) MILITARY LANGUAGE — Imagery of war is used throughout the poem, with the nettles personified as vicious soldiers who attack the boy, are defeated by the father but then rise up again.
4) PAINFUL LANGUAGE — The narrator gives very precise images of the boy's pain, but also links this to the more general pains of growing up.

Remember the Feelings and Attitudes in the Poem

Q7. What kind of plant is this? (2 marks)

1) ANGER — The father's angry at the nettles which hurt his son.
2) REVENGE — He attacks the nettles and tries in a rage to destroy them.
3) FRUSTRATION — He can't permanently remove the cause of his son's pain, and knows that his son will be hurt again and he can't stop it.
4) TENDERNESS — He comforts and takes care of his hurt son.

Go a Step Further and give a Personal Response

Have a go at answering these questions to help you come up with your own ideas about the poem:

Q1.   Why do you think the poet chose to reveal the age of his son?
Q2.   What makes you think the poem is intended as an extended metaphor?
Q3.   Why does the poet include details such as that the nettles are behind the shed, and that he used a hook to cut them down?
Q4.   What does this poem make you think being a parent is like?

Themes — caring for loved ones...

You could compare this poem with 'The Manhunt', to explore how poets portray the difficulties of caring for a loved one. Like 'Born Yesterday', this poem talks about the hopes and fears that adults have for young children. As in 'Sister Maude' there is an angry element.

Philip Larkin

Philip Larkin (1922-1985) was born in Coventry. After graduating from Oxford he spent thirty years working as a librarian for the University of Hull, during which time he produced most of his great works of poetry. In 2008 he was named by The Times newspaper as England's best post-war writer.

Born Yesterday

for Sally Amis

His wish is going to be different from the others.

Tightly-folded bud,
I have wished you something
None of the others would:
Not the usual stuff
5   About being beautiful,
Or running off a spring
Of innocence and love –
They will all wish you that,
And should it prove possible,
10 Well, you're a lucky girl.

Like the beginnings of a flower — image suggests affection which seems to contrast with the hope that she isn't beautiful.

Down-to-earth, unromantic phrase shows his contempt for the supposedly special hopes for a child which are typically expressed.

A source of pure, unpolluted water.

He's cynical and doubts whether these wishes are really likely to come true.

Repetition of negatives — emphasises the absence of distinguishing features.

Repetition in unworkable and working increases the sense that this one extreme thing spreads to disrupt everything else.

Five adjectives in quick succession show how complicated catching happiness is.

But if it shouldn't, then
May you be ordinary;
Have, like other women,
An average of talents:
15 Not ugly, not good-looking,
Nothing uncustomary
To pull you off your balance,
That, unworkable itself,
Stops all the rest from working.
20 In fact, may you be dull –
If that is what a skilled,
Vigilant, flexible,
Unemphasised, enthralled
Catching of happiness is called.

At first his 'unexciting' wishes seem almost unkind.

He explains how this is actually a virtue, more valuable and achievable than those in the first stanza.

Making the last two lines rhyme makes these stand out compared to the more conversational tone of the rest of the poem.

Section One — Poems from the Literary Heritage

Born Yesterday

This poem is about what it really takes to be happy — and it may not quite be what you'd expect from a poet.

You've Got to Know What the Poem's About

If he was any more attractive, he'd fall off.

1) Larkin wrote this poem for a <u>particular event</u> (this is called an occasional piece), the day after the <u>birth</u> of Sally Amis, daughter of his friend Kingsley Amis.

2) He takes the <u>fairy-tale</u> idea of giving out wishes of good things to a newborn, but adds a twist to it by declaring his wish is not for <u>great beauty</u> and <u>exciting things</u>. Instead he wishes her more practical, <u>useful talents</u>.

Learn About the Form, Structure and Language

1) <u>FORM</u> — The lack of rhymes makes most of the poem seem more like <u>normal spoken English</u>, and puts extra <u>emphasis</u> on the rhyming couplet at the end.

2) <u>STRUCTURE</u> — The poet starts off with a conversational and <u>ironic tone</u> talking about the so-called gifts or virtues that most people would wish for a newborn. The second stanza becomes more <u>direct</u> and <u>emphatic</u> towards the end when dealing with the real virtues required to <u>become happy</u>.

3) <u>CYNICAL LANGUAGE</u> — The poet uses <u>sceptical</u> and <u>dismissive</u> language to describe what <u>extraordinary</u> gifts and virtues are worth.

4) <u>LANGUAGE ABOUT ORDINARINESS</u> — The poet gives an <u>unexciting description</u> of his hopes. But he then surprises us with a statement of how <u>important</u> and how <u>special</u> that kind of ordinariness is.

Remember the Feelings and Attitudes in the Poem

1) <u>TENDERNESS</u> — He expresses genuine good feelings for his friend's <u>newborn baby daughter</u>.

2) <u>SCORN</u> — He's quite cutting about the traditional, <u>fairy-tale</u> kind of wishes people make for babies.

3) <u>REALISM</u> — He gives a <u>down-to-earth</u> view of the way people can achieve happiness.

Go a Step Further and give a Personal Response

Have a go at <u>answering</u> these <u>questions</u> to help you come up with <u>your own ideas</u> about the poem:

Q1. What impact does the title have on the meaning of the poem?

Q2. How far do you agree with Larkin's wishes?

Q3. The poem was read out at Sally Amis' funeral. Look up what happened to Sally Amis — does this give the poem an extra resonance which the poet could never have known when he wrote it?

Q4. Many of the poems in this book express how important love is — how is this poem different?

Themes — what's important...

This message links with the ideas of Shakespeare in 'Sonnet 116', that the usual poetic stuff which celebrates outward beauty is not what's really important. Both this poem and 'To His Coy Mistress' talk about the values of others as being unrealistic, wishful thinking.

Simon Armitage

Simon Armitage was born in 1963 in West Yorkshire. As well as poetry, he's also written four stage plays, and writes for TV, film and radio. He studied geography in Portsmouth, and he's now a Senior Lecturer in Creative Writing at Manchester Metropolitan University.

The Manhunt

After the first phase,
after passionate nights and intimate days,

only then would he let me trace
the frozen river which ran through his face,

only then would he let me explore
the blown hinge of his lower jaw,

and handle and hold
the damaged, porcelain collar-bone,

and mind and attend
the fractured rudder of shoulder-blade,

and finger and thumb
the parachute silk of his punctured lung.

Only then could I bind the struts
and climb the rungs of his broken ribs,

and feel the hurt
of his grazed heart.

Skirting along,
only then could I picture the scan,

the foetus of metal beneath his chest
where the bullet had finally come to rest.

Then I widened the search,
traced the scarring back to its source

to a sweating, unexploded mine
buried deep in his mind, around which

every nerve in his body had tightened and closed.
Then, and only then, did I come close.

Suggests she is slowly overcoming his resistance.

The first couplet seems like it could be a normal love poem — as in the first stages of a new relationship.

Repetition of phrases suggests small steps in a slow, painstaking process.

Emphasises how fragile he is and how careful she has to be with him.

The repetition of the structure with two verbs in each stanza emphasises that this is an active process.

Suggests she's patching him up — as if tying his broken ribs back in place.

Parachutes are used by the military — a damaged one would be useless.

Consonance emphasises his emotional pain.

The imagery is as if she has climbed inside him.

She is imagining the scan as being like that for a baby — juxtaposing different images.

Suggests the tension and stress which his memories cause.

The centre of his problems is psychological and emotional.

The last lines only almost rhyme which makes this a muted ending — he's not all better.

Ambiguity — this suggests that she had to wait until now to get "close" to him, but also that she has only "come close".

The Manhunt

This poem shows how the damage war does continues long after the conflict is over.

You've Got to Know What the Poem's About

1) It's written as if spoken by the <u>wife of a soldier</u> who has returned from war with physical scars caused by a bullet which ricocheted through his body.

2) More difficult to see and understand are the <u>mental scars</u> which his experiences have left him with and the <u>problems</u> these are causing.

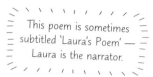
This poem is sometimes subtitled 'Laura's Poem' — Laura is the narrator.

Learn About the Form, Structure and Language

1) <u>FORM</u> — This is a <u>first-person narrative</u> from Laura's viewpoint. The poem is divided into separate <u>couplet-long stanzas</u> which emphasise how this describes a slow, <u>step-by-step</u> process.

2) <u>STRUCTURE</u> — Different <u>injuries</u> are introduced in different <u>couplets</u> — the reader <u>explores</u> the husband's <u>body</u> and <u>mind</u> in the same slow process that his wife has done.

3) <u>LANGUAGE ABOUT THE BODY</u> — His body is described using a range of different <u>adjectives</u> that describe <u>damage</u>, paired with <u>metaphors</u> that suggest his body has become a collection of <u>broken objects</u>. This could be read as suggesting that the damage has <u>taken away</u> some of his <u>humanity</u>.

4) <u>LANGUAGE ABOUT CARING</u> — The poet employs a range of different <u>verbs</u> describing how the woman is <u>caring</u> for the injured man. These words stress <u>carefulness</u> and <u>delicateness</u> which suggest the way in which she <u>cares</u> for him, both <u>physically</u> and <u>emotionally</u>.

Remember the Feelings and Attitudes in the Poem

1) <u>CARING</u> — She is <u>sensitive</u> in her approach to her wounded husband.

2) <u>PATIENCE</u> — It takes the <u>whole poem</u> for the woman to "<u>come close</u>" to her husband.

3) <u>PAIN</u> — The words used to <u>describe</u> the man suggest that his experiences have left him inwardly <u>tormented</u>.

Go a Step Further and give a Personal Response

Have a go at <u>answering</u> these <u>questions</u> to help you come up with <u>your own ideas</u> about the poem:

Q1.   Why do you think the poet has called this poem 'The Manhunt'?

Q2.   How does this poem differ in approach to a news story or a film that you've seen about war?

Q3.   How does this poem make you feel about war? Why?

Themes — pain and suffering...

You could compare this poem to 'Nettles' — they're both on the theme of how people respond to the suffering of a loved one. This poem also gives an example of love continuing in difficult times, which is like the ideal of love in Shakespeare's 'Sonnet 116'.

Carol Ann Duffy

Carol Ann Duffy was born in 1955 in Glasgow. She studied philosophy at the University of Liverpool, and in 1996 began lecturing in poetry at Manchester Metropolitan University. As well as writing poetry, she has also written plays. In 2009 she became the Poet Laureate.

Hour

Love's time's beggar, but even a single hour,
bright as a dropped coin, makes love rich.
We find an hour together, spend it not on flowers
or wine, but the whole of the summer sky and a grass ditch.

5 For thousands of seconds we kiss; your hair
like treasure on the ground; the Midas light
turning your limbs to gold. Time slows, for here
we are millionaires, backhanding the night

so nothing dark will end our shining hour,
10 no jewel hold a candle to the cuckoo spit
hung from the blade of grass at your ear,
no chandelier or spotlight see you better lit

than here. Now. Time hates love, wants love poor,
but love spins gold, gold, gold from straw.

Simile suggests that the hour is more precious for being unexpected. Or alternatively, the hour's like a coin that's been dropped as for a beggar.

Gives the sense of time slowing down — also of cheating time, making it seem more by counting in the smallest division.

The light at sunset makes everything look golden — this might symbolise the way that love makes everything look different.

The single word sentence brings the focus onto the single moment that the poet is trying to capture.

This is what Rumpelstiltskin does in the fairy tale.

Love is dependent on time, but time doesn't need love.

Backhanding suggests bribing as well as pushing back the night.

Through the eyes of the lover everything becomes precious.

Repetition — this adds emphasis to how wonderful this time is, but also perhaps adds to the sense of the time being slowly spun out.

Creating something precious from something ordinary makes it seem like magic.

POEM DICTIONARY
Midas — Mythical ancient Greek king who turned everything he touched into gold
cuckoo spit — white froth found on plants, produced by bugs

Hour

This poem is about how precious time is for lovers. The poet directly addresses her lover, considering the value of their time spent together — however brief.

You've Got to Know What the Poem's About

1) This poem describes an <u>hour</u> spent between the narrator and her lover.
2) The poet <u>personifies</u> time as love's enemy, but in this perfect moment, love almost manages to <u>stop time</u>.

Learn About the Form, Structure and Language

1) <u>FORM</u> — This poem has many of the features of a <u>Shakespearean sonnet</u>, such as the rhyme scheme — but it has <u>varying line lengths</u> and <u>rhythm patterns</u>. The poem is addressed to her lover, which makes it seem <u>direct</u> and <u>intimate</u>. <u>Enjambment</u> between the 2nd and 3rd, and 3rd and 4th stanzas creates pauses that reflect the <u>stopping of time</u> that they are experiencing.

2) <u>STRUCTURE</u> — The poem starts off with two lines on the <u>personification</u> of <u>love</u> and <u>time</u> but mixes this up with memories of a specific afternoon. The <u>final couplet</u> links back to the <u>personified images</u> of <u>time</u> and <u>love</u> in the first stanza — it's made up of words of only <u>one syllable</u> which makes it a <u>forceful</u> and <u>direct</u> ending to quite a <u>dreamy poem</u>.

3) <u>LANGUAGE ABOUT TIME</u> — Time is portrayed as the <u>enemy of love</u>, but also as the <u>currency</u> that love spends. The imagery isn't precise — it suggests the <u>dreamy experience</u> of the lovers.

4) <u>LANGUAGE ABOUT MONEY AND WEALTH</u> — The poem plays with ideas about the <u>value of money</u> compared to <u>time spent together</u>.

Remember the Feelings and Attitudes in the Poem

1) <u>CHERISHING THE MOMENT</u> — Love is felt to be <u>precious</u> and <u>valuable</u>.
2) <u>STRONG BELIEF</u> — The poem expresses faith that love <u>isn't bound by time</u>.
3) <u>PHYSICAL PLEASURE</u> — Love isn't just the idealised, pure devotion of some traditional poems, but also the <u>real</u> and <u>physical</u> — like lying in a ditch, kissing.

"Isn't it time you two got a room?"

Go a Step Further and give a Personal Response

Have a go at <u>answering</u> these <u>questions</u> to help you come up with <u>your own ideas</u> about the poem:

Q1. Midas's gift became a curse to him. Does this affect what you think about the poem?
Q2. Why do you think the poet uses personification in the poem?
Q3. Why do you think the poet wrote this as a form of sonnet?

Themes — love against time...

'Sonnet 116' deals with the relationship between time and love, and also uses personification to do so. Another poem that portrays time as the enemy of love is 'To His Coy Mistress'. You could also compare this poem to 'Sonnet 43' on the theme of the preciousness of love.

James Fenton

James Fenton was born in 1949 in Lincoln. He studied at Magdalen College, Oxford, after which he travelled to East Asia and worked as a political journalist and war correspondent. In 2007 he was awarded the Queen's Gold Medal for Poetry.

In Paris With You

Opening phrase establishes that this is one half of a dialogue and that it's like an anti-love poem.

Trying to appeal to his would-be lover's pity.

War image shows he's being over-dramatic — he feels trapped.

Don't talk to me of love. I've had an earful
And I get tearful when I've downed a drink or two.
I'm one of your talking wounded.
I'm a hostage. I'm maroonded.
5   But I'm in Paris with you.

Suggests he may be a little drunk.

Pun suggests a mix of self pity and self awareness.

Sounds comic — increases the sense that the poem is meant, at least in part, ironically.

Yes I'm angry at the way I've been bamboozled
And resentful at the mess I've been through.
I admit I'm on the rebound
And I don't care where are *we* bound.
10   I'm in Paris with you.

Awkward wording contains the question it's responding to — could be read as responding to or preempting their companion's question. Also makes it into a pun-like rhyme for rebound.

Do you mind if we do *not* go to the Louvre,
If we say sod off to sodding Notre Dame,
If we skip the Champs Elysées
And remain here in this sleazy
15   Old hotel room
Doing this and that
To what and whom
Learning who you are,
Learning what I am.

This could be read as quite careless of the other person — or it could be read as euphemistic.

Paris is known as the city of lovers. Rejecting its most famous landmarks emphasises that this isn't a traditional love poem.

Comic forced rhyme.

This could be read as self reproaching or self absorbed — "what I am" suggests he's lost some of his illusions about himself.

Don't talk to me of love. Let's talk of Paris,
20   The little bit of Paris in our view.
There's that crack across the ceiling
And the hotel walls are peeling
And I'm in Paris with you.

The dingy hotel could be read as reflecting his emotional state and the nature of their relationship.

Looking at the ceiling may suggest lying on your back.

Don't talk to me of love. Let's talk of Paris.
25   I'm in Paris with the slightest thing you do.
I'm in Paris with your eyes, your mouth,
I'm in Paris with… all points south.
Am I embarrassing you?
30   I'm in Paris with you.

Suggests genuine attraction and close attention.

This is quite humorous but also makes clear what he is after.

Could be teasing or sympathetic.

In Paris With You

Paris — city of romance, city of lovers... and city of broken-hearted poets with little interest in where are we bound.

You've Got to Know What the Poem's About

1) The speaker in the poem is <u>upset</u> about love. He sees himself as a <u>victim</u> following the <u>breakdown</u> of a relationship.

2) He's gone to <u>Paris</u> with someone else, but still seems <u>unhappy</u> and <u>discontented</u>. He doesn't want to <u>go out</u> into the <u>city</u> — he'd rather <u>stay</u> in the <u>hotel room</u>.

Learn About the Form, Structure and Language

1) <u>FORM</u> — The poem is made up of one main <u>repeating stanza pattern</u>, with a very <u>different third stanza</u> which makes it <u>stand out</u>. The poem is structured in quite a <u>songlike</u> way, with lots of <u>repetition</u>, including the <u>main refrain</u>, and <u>internal rhymes</u> to emphasise the rhythm.

2) <u>STRUCTURE</u> — The first stanzas are about the <u>narrator</u>, then the focus shifts to <u>Paris</u>. The third stanza is <u>structured differently</u> and is where he <u>signals his intent</u>. The penultimate verse turns the attention to their <u>surroundings</u> and the final verse onto his <u>companion</u> — it ends with a more <u>assertive</u> than <u>self-pitying</u> tone.

3) <u>LANGUAGE ABOUT PARIS</u> — The idea of being <u>in Paris</u> is very important in the poem and he names some of the <u>most important landmarks</u> — but suggests they avoid them. Paris is often associated with romance — but in this context it seems <u>partly ironic</u> as his thoughts <u>aren't</u> very <u>romantic</u>.

4) <u>HUMOROUS LANGUAGE</u> — Nearly every stanza contains either a <u>contrived</u> or an <u>unexpected rhyme</u>. He also keeps repeating the word <u>Paris</u>, while reducing it to the inside of a <u>grotty hotel room</u>.

Remember the Feelings and Attitudes in the Poem

1) <u>SELF-PITY</u> — He starts the poem very focused on his own <u>misery</u>.

2) <u>BITTERNESS</u> — He's very <u>resentful</u> about the breakdown of his previous relationship.

3) <u>HUMOUR</u> — He's self-pitying, but the <u>puns</u> and <u>unexpected rhymes</u> suggest humour.

4) <u>LUST</u> — He makes his intentions <u>very clear</u>.

"Sorry — can't be bothered."

Go a Step Further and give a Personal Response

Have a go at <u>answering</u> these <u>questions</u> to help you come up with <u>your own ideas</u> about the poem:

Q1.   How would you describe the narrator's mood at the beginning of the poem, and at the end?

Q2.   What is the effect of humour in the poem? Do you think that the poem is more funny or sad?

Q3.   Why do you think the word Paris is repeated so often?

Q4.   Would it change what you thought of the poem if the narrator was a woman rather than a man?

Themes — bad feelings...

The narrator starts this poem very bitterly — you could compare these bad feelings to the anger expressed in 'Sister Maude' and the sense of being hurt in 'Quickdraw'. 'To His Coy Mistress' also features a narrator trying to seduce someone, and it's another poem that uses humour.

Carol Ann Duffy

<u>Carol Ann Duffy</u> was born in 1955 in Glasgow. She studied philosophy at the University of Liverpool, and in 1996 began lecturing in poetry at Manchester Metropolitan University. As well as writing poetry, she has also written plays. In 2009 she became the Poet Laureate.

Quickdraw

Enjambment gives emphasis to the word by leaving it alone on the line away from the rest of its sentence.

I wear the two, the mobile and the landline phones,
like guns, slung from the pockets on my hips. I'm all
alone. You ring, quickdraw, your voice a pellet
in my ear, and hear me groan.

Suggests how rapidly she answers the phone.

Rhyme links this word with "alone" on previous line.

Split lines suggest just how hurt she is by the lover's words.

5   You've wounded me.
Next time, you speak after the tone. I twirl the phone,
then squeeze the trigger of my tongue, wide of the mark.
You choose your spot, then blast me

Internal rhyme adds emphasis to the fractured rhythm of the poem.

Enjambment makes the poem seem less structured and perhaps more breathless.

                                              through the heart.
10 And this is love, high noon, calamity, hard liquor
in the old Last Chance saloon. I show the mobile
to the Sheriff; in my boot, another one's

A classic western image, but also suggests a relationship that is close to the end.

It's like she's been shot and also links the events with films.

concealed. You text them both at once. I reel.
Down on my knees, I fumble for the phone,
15 read the silver bullets of your kiss. Take this ...
and this ... and this ... and this ... and this ...

Sounds precious and valuable.

The repetition makes it seem that these texted kisses are like bullets fired from a gun.

<u>Quickdraw</u>

This poem is about a difficult relationship — but still a tense and exciting one.

<u>You've Got to Know *What the Poem's About*</u>

1) This poem compares the <u>phone calls</u> and <u>texts</u> in a relationship to a <u>gun fight</u> in a <u>Western</u>.
2) The <u>narrator</u> of the poem seems to get the <u>worst</u> of these encounters, and is left <u>hurt</u> and <u>wounded</u>.
3) What finally finishes the narrator off isn't <u>cruelty</u> but a series of text message <u>kisses</u> which strike her like <u>bullets</u>.

<u>Learn About the *Form, Structure and Language*</u>

1) <u>FORM</u> — This poem is very <u>loosely structured</u>. This adds to the <u>tension</u> as we don't know what to expect next, just as the narrator doesn't. The poem is littered with <u>enjambment</u>, <u>assonance</u>, <u>alliteration</u> and <u>internal rhymes</u> at <u>irregular intervals</u>, which helps make the poem seem <u>tense</u> and <u>unpredictable</u>.
2) <u>STRUCTURE</u> — The poem describes how the lover <u>makes contact</u> a series of times, and the narrator's <u>reactions</u>. We experience the events in <u>the order</u> the narrator does, adding to the <u>tension</u>.
3) <u>LANGUAGE ABOUT COMMUNICATION</u> — The poem describes communication by <u>phone</u> and by <u>text</u>. Text messages and mobile phones — being relatively <u>recent inventions</u> — don't feature in much poetry, which helps this to seem <u>modern</u> and <u>different</u>.
4) <u>LANGUAGE FROM WESTERNS</u> — The poem contains quite <u>clichéd imagery</u> taken from <u>TV</u> and <u>cinema</u>. The <u>old-fashioned</u> imagery <u>contrasts</u> with the references to <u>mobile phones</u> and <u>text messaging</u>.

<u>Remember the *Feelings and Attitudes in the Poem*</u>

"Put your hands up, sweetheart."

1) <u>HURT</u> — The Western imagery makes the <u>pains</u> of being in a relationship seem quite <u>physical</u> — <u>knocking her down</u> in the final stanza.
2) <u>EXPECTATION</u> — Despite the <u>pain</u> that the relationship is causing her the narrator seems <u>desperate</u> to get the messages — answering the phone <u>quickly</u> in the first stanza and <u>fumbling</u> for it in the final one.
3) <u>TENSION</u> — The narrator seems <u>on edge</u> throughout the poem.

<u>Go a *Step Further* and give a *Personal Response*</u>

Have a go at <u>answering</u> these <u>questions</u> to help you come up with <u>your own ideas</u> about the poem:

Q1.   Who do you think the Sheriff might be?
Q2.   What do you think about the image of kisses being like bullets?
Q3.   Other than giving the idea of bullets from a gun, what impact does the repetition in the final line have?

Themes — attitudes towards love...

Sometimes romantic love involves people getting hurt — which is something this poem, 'The Farmer's Bride' and 'In Paris With You' all deal with. You could also talk about the theme of communication in this poem, which is also dealt with, in a very different way, in 'The Manhunt'.

Section Two — Contemporary Poems

Mimi Khalvati

Mimi Khalvati was born in 1944 in Tehran. She went to boarding school on the Isle of Wight, then studied in London. She founded The Poetry School, where she is now a tutor, and has worked as an actor and director in the UK and Iran.

Ghazal

Repetition — the lover is trying out different scenarios on her beloved.

If I am the grass and you the breeze, blow through me.
If I am the rose and you the bird, then woo me.

Suggests she wants him to be firm but also gentle with her.

If you are the rhyme and I the refrain, don't hang
on my lips, come and I'll come too when you cue me.

The enjambment reflects her waiting for the "cue" on the next line.

5   If yours is the iron fist in the velvet glove
when the arrow flies, the heart is pierced, tattoo me.

A heart pierced with an arrow is a traditional tattoo.

She wants him to be like a snake charmer — teasing and in control.

If mine is the venomous tongue, the serpent's tail,
charmer, use your charm, weave a spell and subdue me.

A dangerous animal — the natural imagery she uses to describe herself isn't tame or gentle.

If I am the laurel leaf in your crown, you are
10   the arms around my bark, arms that never knew me.

Oh would that I were bark! So old and still in leaf.
And you, dropping in my shade, dew to bedew me!

This question could be read as summing up the whole poem.

What shape should I take to marry your own, have you
– hawk to my shadow, moth to my flame – pursue me?

She wants to get him to be the active one in the relationship.

Like the sun and moon setting and rising in turn.

15   If I rise in the east as you die in the west,
die for my sake, my love, every night renew me.

This is quite a different idea from one you find in most traditional love poetry.

If, when it ends, we are just good friends, be my Friend,
muse, lover and guide, Shamsuddin to my Rumi.

Be heaven and earth to me and I'll be twice the me
20   I am, if only half the world you are to me.

Ghazals traditionally feature the poet's name in the last stanza, often through a play on words — "twice the me" is Mimi.

POEM DICTIONARY
refrain — a line that is repeated in poetry or song
laurel — laurel leaves in a wreath are traditional symbols of victory
bedew — make something wet — like dew
muse — someone who inspires an artist
Shamsuddin — or Shams Tabrizi, the mystical friend and mentor of Rumi
Rumi — important religious figure and poet. He was close friends with Shams (or Shamsuddin) —
        when Shams disappeared Rumi was inspired to write mystical poetry.

Ghazal

This poem uses a very old form to declare the feelings of the narrator for a loved one. No one's ever written me a poem.

You've Got to Know What the Poem's About

1) In this poem the writer expresses <u>intense feelings of love</u>.
2) She conjures up a <u>new image</u>, or number of images, in <u>each stanza</u>.

Learn About the Form, Structure and Language

1) <u>FORM</u> — A <u>ghazal</u> is an ancient poetic form originally from the <u>Middle East</u>, often used to express the <u>beauty</u> and <u>pains</u> of love. The <u>final word</u> in each couplet is the <u>same</u>, but the <u>last-but-one words</u> in each stanza <u>also rhyme</u> with each other. The couplets <u>aren't supposed</u> to be <u>connected</u> as in a narrative.
2) <u>STRUCTURE</u> — The <u>separate</u> nature of each stanza means that we are given a <u>whole range</u> of <u>different</u> <u>ideas</u> and <u>images</u> in <u>quick succession</u>. This makes this poem seem <u>playful</u> but also <u>quite intense</u>.
3) <u>LANGUAGE ABOUT NATURE</u> — Using <u>natural imagery</u> makes the poem seem <u>timeless</u> — suggesting her love is <u>permanent</u> and profound. This also presents their love as a <u>natural thing</u>.
4) <u>LANGUAGE ABOUT BEING LOVED</u> — She is asking to be the <u>object</u> of her lover's love, despite the fact that she is the one <u>chasing him</u> with this poem. The language in the poem makes clear her love isn't all about sweetness — some of the images carry hints of <u>conflict</u> or <u>aggression</u>.

Remember the Feelings and Attitudes in the Poem

1) <u>INTENSE LOVE</u> — She seems to love almost to the <u>point of obsession</u>.
2) <u>PLAYFULNESS</u> — The range of <u>different images</u> and the <u>repeating rhymes</u> make this seem a <u>joyous</u> and <u>playful</u> poem.
3) <u>PLEASURE</u> — The narrator seems to <u>enjoy</u> being in love and the <u>language of love</u>.

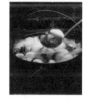

"If I am the beef, potatoes, carrots and cabbage, and you the simmering stock..."

Go a Step Further and give a Personal Response

Have a go at <u>answering</u> these <u>questions</u> to help you come up with <u>your own ideas</u> about the poem:

Q1. What do you think the poet is searching for in these verses?
Q2. What title would you give to this ghazal?
Q3. What does the poem reveal about the person it was written to?
Q4. Do any of these images suggest to you a darker side to love? How?

Themes — attitudes towards love...

This poem uses a lot of natural imagery, which you could use to connect it to 'The Farmer's Bride', 'Nettles' and 'Hour'. It's a poem that conveys a sense of physical desire, which you could look at in relation to 'To His Coy Mistress' or 'Hour'.

Andrew Forster

<u>Andrew Forster</u> was born in South Yorkshire. His first poetry collection, 'Fear of Thunder', was published in 2007.

Brothers

First word emphasises his frustration.

Alliteration gives a sense of the contempt he feels at this moment for his brother, whose views are worthless because of his age.

Language suggesting innocent joy.

The older two move more slowly and with confidence.

It's not clear if he can't or simply doesn't want to.

Alliteration — emphasises how ridiculous he thinks the younger child's views are.

Rotherham are a less fashionable club than Sheffield Wednesday.

Contrast between how young they are and how grown up they feel at the time.

Their sense of assumed maturity.

Conveys their sense of physical prowess that the younger one lacks — but also the imagination of children.

Shows he is now too far away to see.

Ambiguous — both the physical distance between them and a distance in their relationship.

Saddled with you for the afternoon, me and Paul
ambled across the threadbare field to the bus stop,
talking over Sheffield Wednesday's chances in the Cup
while you skipped beside us in your ridiculous tank-top,
5   spouting six-year-old views on Rotherham United.

Suddenly you froze, said you hadn't any bus fare.
I sighed, said you should go and ask Mum
and while you windmilled home I looked at Paul.
His smile, like mine, said I was nine and he was ten
10   and we must stroll the town, doing what grown-ups do.

As a bus crested the hill we chased Olympic Gold.
Looking back I saw you spring towards the gate,
your hand holding out what must have been a coin.
I ran on, unable to close the distance I'd set in motion.

Brothers

This is a poem about an event in the narrator's childhood — but it can also be read as being about sibling relationships in general. Personally, I blame the parents.

You've Got to Know What the Poem's About

1) In the poem the narrator remembers a <u>moment</u> from his <u>childhood</u>. He and <u>his elder brother</u> are given the <u>responsibility</u> of looking after their <u>younger brother</u> for the afternoon.

2) They are <u>exasperated</u> with him — but <u>excited</u> to be out on their own.

3) They send their younger brother back to get his <u>bus fare</u> from their mother. But then they <u>run on</u>, leaving him behind.

Learn About the Form, Structure and Language

1) <u>FORM</u> — This is a <u>narrative poem</u> addressed to the six-year-old in the poem, seemingly some years after the events they describe. This poem is written in <u>free verse</u>, making it seem more like a story being told in <u>spoken English</u>.

2) <u>STRUCTURE</u> — The first stanza establishes the <u>relationship</u> between the brothers. The second explains how the youngest had to <u>go back</u> and how the older two <u>went on</u>. The third stanza describes how the youngest got <u>left behind</u>, and hints at the <u>impact</u> this may have had.

3) <u>LANGUAGE ABOUT YOUTH</u> — Much of the poem contrasts the younger child's <u>youthful exuberance</u> with the older brothers' sense of <u>self-possession</u> and <u>maturity</u> — which is still mixed with the <u>imagination</u> of children.

4) <u>LANGUAGE ABOUT MATURITY</u> — The older two think they're mature because they talk and act confidently — but the poem is written with the <u>hindsight</u> of actual maturity, and sees that this was a <u>bad moment</u> for their relationship.

Remember the Feelings and Attitudes in the Poem

1) <u>FRUSTRATION</u> — The narrator and Paul want to <u>get away</u> from the younger child.

2) <u>GUILT</u> — The narrator presents his younger sibling as <u>eager</u>, using <u>childlike</u>, innocent terms. This makes the narrator's actions seem <u>worse</u>.

3) <u>REGRET</u> — The poem suggests that, even at the time, <u>part of him</u> wanted to go back, and he wishes that he could close the "<u>distance</u>" in his relationship with his younger sibling.

If only she'd remembered to give Timmy his bus fare, this could all have been avoided.

Go a Step Further and give a Personal Response

Have a go at <u>answering</u> these <u>questions</u> to help you come up with <u>your own ideas</u> about the poem:

Q1. What difference would it make to what you think of the poem if the younger sibling is a sister?

Q2. Why do you think the poet chose to call this poem 'Brothers'?

Q3. What does the last line suggest about how the relationship developed after this event?

Themes — family relationships...

This poem is about an unhappy event in the relationship between brothers — for an angrier, more violent version between sisters you could always look at 'Sister Maude'. Like 'Nettles', this is a poem that reflects back on an incident relating to childhood.

Grace Nichols

Grace Nichols was born in Guyana in 1950. She was a teacher and journalist in the Caribbean until she moved to Britain in 1977. Both of these cultures and how they interlink are important to her.

Praise Song For My Mother

You were
water to me
deep and bold and fathoming

You were
5   moon's eye to me
pull and grained and mantling

You were
sunrise to me
rise and warm and streaming

10   You were
the fish's red gill to me
the flame tree's spread to me
the crab's leg/the fried plantain smell
            replenishing replenishing

15   Go to your wide futures, you said

The moon pulls the tides — suggests an influence that isn't forced.

This stanza has a lot more precise imagery than the previous stanzas.

Suggests boundless possibilities — emigration?

The adjectives used to describe her mother are not straightforward — her mother's love was more than can be captured in everyday language.

Double meaning — suggests both depth and understanding.

Repetition gives the sense of being formal verse — she isn't trying to express herself in everyday spoken English.

These smells merge into one.

Repetition suggests this is an ongoing process, not a single event — or even a collection of events.

POEM DICTIONARY
fathoming — to get to the bottom of something or to measure the depth of something
grained — textured like the surface of wood
mantling — to cover or wrap up — a mantle is a type of cloak
plantain — a banana-like food from the Caribbean

Praise Song For My Mother

This is a poem all about how great someone's mother is. Just think, without Grace Nichols's mum, you'd be looking at a couple of blank pages. Cheers Mrs N.

You've Got to Know What the Poem's About

1) The poem brings up different aspects of a mother-daughter relationship, showing how the mother was like a complete world to her child.

2) The mother is likened to water, the moon (night), sunrise (day) and food — a mixture of the necessities of life along with the days and nights in which it's lived.

Learn About the Form, Structure and Language

1) FORM — Each of the first three stanzas follows the same pattern of describing what the mother was to her using a different image.

2) STRUCTURE — The poem doesn't develop a story or narrative, and is largely unpunctuated — this suggests how the good memories have merged into one warm picture. It also suggests that this poem isn't about a single event, but the experiences of many years.

3) LANGUAGE ABOUT HER MOTHER — The poem has words in it that wouldn't normally be used to describe a loved one — these suggest that the poet has gone beyond the traditional form and that this is meant to be heartfelt rather than formulaic. Many of these words are out of their usual context and don't have one simple meaning — making us see the mother's importance as beyond simple explanations.

4) LANGUAGE ABOUT FOOD — The types of food described are eaten in the Caribbean, linking the mother to a specific place and emphasising how her mother was a nourishing presence. The final stanza can be read as describing a meal. It covers seeing the fish, feeling the shelter of the tree and the smell of the food — this suggests how her mother's presence touched all her senses.

Remember the Feelings and Attitudes in the Poem

You were chicken burgers to me — thanks Mum.

1) GRATITUDE — The poem is expressing her thanks for her mother's love and support.

2) JOY — The memories she has of her mother are warm and joyful ones.

3) PRAISE — This song gives her the chance to tell everyone how she feels about her mother.

Go a Step Further and give a Personal Response

Have a go at answering these questions to help you come up with your own ideas about the poem:

Q1.   What do you think the image of sunrise suggests about how the narrator sees her mother?

Q2.   What can you learn about the mother's feelings for her daughter?

Q3.   Why do you think the poet makes food so important in the poem?

Themes — parental love...

You could compare this poem with 'Harmonium', which is also about the narrator's relationship with a parent. 'Nettles' looks at the same theme from the perspective of the parent rather than their offspring. You could also look at how this poem and 'Ghazal' use natural imagery.

Simon Armitage

Simon Armitage was born in 1963 in West Yorkshire. As well as poetry, he's also written four stage plays, and writes for TV, film and radio. He studied geography in Portsmouth, and he's now a Senior Lecturer in Creative Writing at Manchester Metropolitan University.

The make of the harmonium and the location of the church make clear this is an event the poet wants us to believe actually happened.

Pun — both that he got it cheaply and that he can use it for singing.

Suggests atmosphere of the church, perhaps also the pictures in the windows.

Onomatopoeia — mimicking the sound of the harmonium emphasised by the alliteration.

This lively image stands out from the ordinariness of the rest of the poem.

Suggests age and ill-health — links his tobacco stained fingers to the yellowed keys of the harmonium.

Internal rhyme suggests father's dark humour.

Harmonium

The *Farrand Chapelette* was gathering dust
in the shadowy porch of Marsden Church.
And was due to be bundled off to the skip.
Or was mine, for a song, if I wanted it.

5   Sunlight, through stained glass, which day to day
could beatify saints and raise the dead,
had aged the harmonium's softwood case
and yellowed the fingernails of its keys.
And one of its notes had lost its tongue,
10   and holes were worn in both the treadles
where the organist's feet, in grey, woollen socks
and leather-soled shoes, had pedalled and pedalled.

But its hummed harmonics still struck a chord:
for a hundred years that organ had stood
15   by the choristers' stalls, where father and son,
each in their time, had opened their throats
and gilded finches – like high notes – had streamed out.

Through his own blue cloud of tobacco smog,
with smoker's fingers and dottled thumbs,
20   he comes to help me cart it away.
And we carry it flat, laid on its back.
And he, being him, can't help but say
that the next box I'll shoulder through this nave
will bear the freight of his own dead weight.
25   And I, being me, then mouth in reply
some shallow or sorry phrase or word
too starved of breath to make itself heard.

Unused and neglected.

Unromantic language — suggests being treated like any other rubbish.

Personifies the harmonium — it's described like an ageing person.

Ordinary, everyday description.

Repetition emphasises the passing of time.

Pun — can play chords and still appeals.

Thinking of all the generations who've sung here leads him to think of his own relationship.

Reverses the usual order of the simile.

A reference to the way a body is carried in a coffin for a funeral.

Last two lines rhyme — adding extra emphasis. For all that age and time have done to the harmonium and his father, it is the narrator left speechless and breathless.

POEM DICTIONARY
harmonium — a type of organ which was often found in small churches, operated by pumping two treadles
Marsden — a village in West Yorkshire
beatify — declare someone's holiness or make very happy
treadle — a lever you work with your foot
gilded — covered with a layer of gold

Harmonium

...in which the narrator heads off to a small church to pick up a church organ.
You heard it here first.

You've Got to Know *What* the Poem's *About*

1) The narrator and his father (or an old friend or relative) are picking
   up a <u>harmonium</u> that he's <u>bought cheaply</u> from a church.

2) He reflects on how the <u>passage of time</u> has affected the instrument
   — and the <u>years of service</u> it has given in the church.

3) His father is <u>helping him</u> take the harmonium away. His father makes a <u>joke</u>
   about <u>death</u> which seems to make the narrator uncomfortable.

Learn About the *Form, Structure and Language*

1) <u>FORM</u> — The use of <u>free verse</u> makes this poem close to <u>ordinary speech</u>, as if the poet
   were <u>telling a story</u>. This gives a sense that these events <u>actually occurred</u>.

2) <u>STRUCTURE</u> — The poem <u>starts off</u> by explaining how he came by the harmonium. The
   <u>second stanza</u> talks about how the harmonium <u>appears now</u>, the third stanza about <u>its past</u> in
   the church. The last stanza is about the <u>relationship</u> between the narrator and his father.

3) <u>LANGUAGE ABOUT ORDINARINESS</u> — Much of the language is quite <u>unromantic</u> —
   which <u>sets the scene</u> and contrasts with the <u>spiritual use</u> of the harmonium.

4) <u>LANGUAGE ABOUT THE PASSING OF TIME</u> — The <u>effects of time</u> are described through the <u>damage</u> to the
   harmonium. The poem <u>links</u> the fate of the harmonium to that of the <u>father</u>, who jokes about his death.

5) <u>HUMOROUS LANGUAGE</u> — This poem contains a number of <u>puns</u> — but when the
   father makes a joke about <u>his own death</u> the narrator doesn't respond well.

Remember the *Feelings and Attitudes in the Poem*

1) <u>SPEECHLESSNESS</u> — The narrator feels awkward and
   has <u>no response</u> to talk of his father's death.

2) <u>HUMOUR</u> — This is quite a <u>bleak poem</u>, but the narrator makes <u>puns</u>
   about the harmonium and the father <u>jokes</u> about his own death.

3) <u>SADNESS</u> — The poem deals with the idea of <u>death</u> and the <u>effects of time</u>.

Check out the treadles
on this one.

Go a *Step Further* and give a *Personal Response*

Have a go at <u>answering</u> these <u>questions</u> to help you come up with <u>your own ideas</u> about the poem:

Q1.   Why does the poet mention his father's fingers and thumbs, and the organist's feet?

Q2.   What does the imagery in line 17 make you think of?

Q3.   What impact does the phase "too starved of breath" have on your reading of the poem?

Q4.   Why do you think he wants the harmonium?

Themes — unhappiness...

'Harmonium' deals with how family relationships, even when they're generally good ones,
can be a source of unhappiness. Another poem that touches upon a similar theme is
'Nettles', which looks at similar themes from the other side of the father-son relationship.

Relationships

All of the poems in this book cover the theme of relationships. In the exam you'll be expected to be able to make links between these poems.

> 1) Relationships are the connections between two or more people.
> 2) There are romantic relationships, family relationships, and the relationships you have with your friends.

People can have Different Feelings about each other

To His Coy Mistress (Pages 6-7)

1) The narrator wants to have a <u>physical relationship</u> with his mistress — "let us sport us while we may" — but she seems to need <u>some persuasion</u>.
2) There's a sense of <u>frustration</u> in the poem that the narrator wants his mistress to think <u>as he does</u>.

Somehow they remained great friends — despite having different feelings about skinny dipping.

The Farmer's Bride (Pages 8-9)

1) The farmer wants to be able to <u>touch</u> and <u>love</u> his bride, but she is <u>really scared</u> of him — "'Not near, not near!' her eyes beseech".
2) The farmer still sees her as <u>attractive</u>, but the things he says about her link her to the world of <u>animals</u> rather than <u>people</u>. He views her with a mixture of <u>sadness</u> and <u>desire</u>.
3) She seems to see him only as a <u>threat</u>.

People in a relationship can feel Protective

The Manhunt (Pages 18-19)

1) The ex-soldier's wife <u>isn't put off</u> by her husband's shattered body and emotions. She wants to "bind the struts" and help him <u>come to terms</u> with what happened to him.
2) She shows <u>affection</u>, <u>dedication</u> and <u>loyalty</u> in sticking with her husband through difficult times.

Nettles (Pages 14-15)

1) The father really wishes he could <u>protect</u> his son, not just from the nettles, which he "slashed in fury" but also from the <u>pains in life</u>.
2) This suggests that in parenthood there will always be the <u>sadness</u> of knowing that as much as people may want to <u>spare</u> their children pain, <u>everyone suffers</u> as they go through life.

Born Yesterday (Pages 16-17)

1) The narrator wants Sally to have the "<u>talents</u>" needed to be <u>happy</u> in life.
2) He suggests that she needs to be <u>protected</u> from the pressure of being <u>too talented</u> or <u>attractive</u>, as these attributes can come at the price of <u>taking away happiness</u>.

There are other poems which touch on these themes...

Differences in feelings can sometimes even lead to outright aggression and hostility — like in the western gunfight-style imagery describing the lovers in 'Quickdraw'. In 'Brothers' the two older brothers feel exasperated with their younger brother, but he seems excited to be out with them.

Relationships

Relationships aren't always about sweetness and light.

Sometimes people can be Mean and Cruel

Sister Maude (Pages 12-13)

1) The narrator wants her sister to <u>suffer</u> for telling her parents about her relationship — "But sister Maude shall get no sleep".
2) She aims to <u>hurt</u> her sister by telling her that the young man would never have fancied her anyway — "He'd never have looked at you".
3) This poem highlights the extra <u>tensions</u> that can occur in <u>sibling relationships</u>. <u>Rivalries</u> and <u>disagreements</u> can be more <u>intense</u> as the relationship is so close.

Quickdraw (Pages 24-25)

1) The unpleasant telephone call and texts from her lover <u>really upset</u> the character in this poem — "You choose your spot, then blast me / through the heart".
2) By making their relationship seem like a gunfight, she shows the element of <u>competition</u> and <u>combat</u> in romantic relationships, which can get <u>overlooked</u> in some <u>more traditional</u> views of love.

"LOL?" — "LMAO."

Some people are just Inconsiderate

In Paris With You (Pages 22-23)

1) In his own misery at a previous, failed relationship, the narrator is <u>insensitive</u> to the feelings of the person he's now with — "I don't care where are *we* bound".
2) His feelings show how a <u>negative end</u> to one relationship can have a <u>bad effect</u> on future relationships.
3) Or you could argue that this relationship's helping him <u>get over</u> the old one. The poem moves from a maudlin look at the <u>damage</u> the old relationship's done, to a more <u>lustful</u> and <u>outgoing engagement</u> with the other person.

Brothers (Pages 28-29)

1) The older children <u>don't go back</u> for their younger sibling. The narrator recognises in the poem this was a <u>mean</u> thing to do, hinting at the <u>regret</u> he feels — "I ran on, unable to close the distance I'd set in motion."
2) This shows the way that the <u>tensions</u> in family relationships often go back to <u>childhood</u>, to events that may have seemed <u>trivial</u> at the time.

> There are a wide range of different relationships in this selection, which span some 400 years of poetry writing. Remember, none of them were written to fit with each other — the links you make between them are your links.

Other poems feature the theme of bad feelings...

For example, in 'The Farmer's Bride' the bride is filled with terror when faced with her husband.

Negative Emotions

Relationships often involve negative emotions. E.g. "I'm angry — my sister's an idiot" and "I used to like that boy, but I am disgusted by his smelly dog."

1) Relationships bring out a range of emotions in people — not just happy ones.

2) Jealousy, anger and guilt are emotions that often rise up between people when relationships turn sour.

People can be very Bitter

In Paris With You (Pages 22-23)

1) The narrator is very bitter. He resents the breakdown of his previous relationship — "I'm angry at the way I've been bamboozled".
2) He doesn't really seem to give the new relationship much of a chance — "Don't talk to me of love".
3) He starts the poem sunk in self-pity — "I get tearful".
4) It's almost as though he's enjoying wallowing in his misery.

Sister Maude (Pages 12-13)

1) The narrator is furious with her sister for telling her parents about her lover — "Who told my mother of my shame".
2) She sees her sister as a sneak and a tell-tale — "Who lurked to spy and peer."
3) She wants her sister to suffer for what she did — "Bide *you* with death and sin."
4) Because this is a dramatic monologue, we only get the bitter view of the unhappy sister.

Some people feel Regret and other Negative Emotions

Brothers (Pages 28-29)

1) The writer presents his younger brother as eager, innocent and childlike — "you skipped beside us".
2) But at the time the narrator was impatient and frustrated at being "saddled" with him.
3) In contrast to his younger brother, he thought that he knew it all — "doing what grown-ups do".
4) Looking back, he seems to know now that he made a really bad decision by leaving the youngster behind.
5) It seems to have caused a rift between them which he blames himself for — "the distance I'd set in motion".

The Farmer's Bride (Pages 8-9)

1) The farmer seems to feel uncomfortable about his desire for his young bride who has rejected his advances.
2) There is a suggestion that the farmer may be jealous of the animals his wife talks to — "I've hardly heard her speak at all."
3) His exclamation "Oh! my God!" and the repetition "the brown / The brown of her — her eyes, her hair, her hair!" suggest how he struggles to control his desire.

Other poems feature negative emotions...

'Nettles', 'The Manhunt' and 'Harmonium' are all downbeat poems — focusing on the fact that relationships, even good ones, may contain an element of unhappiness.

Love

Relationships aren't just about love — but it is a big part of it. However, you and I have a working relationship, so any feelings you may have for me would be completely inappropriate.

> 1) A lot of poetry is written about love — not surprising as it's one of the most intense feelings we can have.
> 2) Love for family members and for lovers can be complicated.

Some poems are about Romantic Love

The Manhunt (Pages 18-19)

1) The injured soldier has a loving relationship with his wife, who isn't put off by his wounds.
2) The poet refers to their relationship as "passionate" and "intimate" in the first stanza. This tells the reader how important that part of their relationship is.
3) Laura tries to understand what happened to her husband. At first she does this by tentatively exploring his physical wounds and scars — "hold / the damaged, porcelain collar-bone".
4) She then tries to understand the emotional damage that has been done to him — "I widened the search" to an "unexploded mine / buried deep in his mind".

"We both love looking at saucy postcards"

Hour (Pages 20-21)

1) Duffy uses personification to explore both the physical and spiritual sides of love — "Love's time's beggar".
2) She uses imagery of precious things to reflect how much she values her love — "treasure", "gold", "jewel".
3) At the end she rejoices in how wonderful love is, using repetition to emphasise this — "love spins gold, gold, gold from straw."

Ghazal (Pages 26-27)

1) The love presented is so intense it sometimes seems painful — "when the arrow flies, the heart is pierced".
2) Other times, imagery of nature is used to show the pleasure and joy in loving and in being loved — "If I am the grass and you the breeze, blow through me."

Some poems are about the love of Parents for their Children

Praise Song For My Mother (Pages 30-31)

1) Writing the poem is an opportunity for the narrator to share the gratitude she feels for the incredible strength of her mother's love for her — "You were / sunrise to me".
2) She uses the Praise Song to celebrate her mother's constant, giving love. She uses one line offset from the others to reinforce this message — "replenishing replenishing".
3) Having given her this wonderful childhood, the mother sent her off to explore her own potential, without wanting her to feel guilty for leaving — "Go to your wide futures, you said".

Other poems feature the theme of love...

You could contrast any of the more romantic poems with 'In Paris With You', 'The Farmer's Bride' or 'Quickdraw' to show that love isn't always nice.

Time

Poets often like to reflect on time. Maybe it's because they've got so much of it to spare...

> 1) Relationships are all about time — spent together, spent apart, spent growing up, and spent growing old.
> 2) Time is often seen as something that threatens love — damaging the loved one and often taking them away.

Time spent Together is seen as Precious

Hour (Pages 20-21)

1) The poet uses images of <u>valuable things</u> to show how important <u>time</u> spent with her lover is — "we are millionaires".
2) She <u>personifies</u> time to make it seem the <u>enemy</u> of love — "Time hates love, wants love poor".
3) The <u>fairy-tale image</u> of straw being spun into gold suggests that love can <u>triumph</u> over time.

People look back Fondly on time spent with Loved Ones

Praise Song For My Mother (Pages 30-31)

1) The narrator <u>really values</u> the time that her mother gave to her when she was growing up — "You were / sunrise to me".
2) She sees her mother as a <u>nourishing</u> presence, giving her a wonderful, colourful childhood of endless love — "warm and streaming".
3) Her mother knew when it was time for the narrator to <u>move away</u> and <u>explore</u> her own <u>potential</u> — "Go to your wide futures, you said".
4) This suggests how <u>good memories</u> can give <u>confidence</u> for the future.

No time for love — too busy clowning.

Some poets think that love can last Forever

Sonnet 43 (Pages 10-11)

1) In this poem the narrator suggests that <u>love</u> can survive death into <u>eternity</u>.
2) You could also argue that she believes love is powerful enough to <u>transcend time</u> and bring back <u>emotions</u> from the past — "I shall but love thee better after death".
3) It seems as if this love has influenced and affected her <u>whole life</u>. This could be read as <u>changing</u> how she feels about the <u>time before</u> they met — "I love thee with the breath, / Smiles, tears, of all my life!"

Other poems feature the theme of time...

In 'To His Coy Mistress' the narrator tries to get his mistress to be more amorous and adventurous by reminding her that time is passing. 'Harmonium' looks at how the passage of time has damaged the harmonium, but also reflects on time's painful effects on loved ones.

Getting Older

You can't avoid getting older. It's not all bad — just think, one
day you'll be old enough to choose your own poems.

> An inevitable effect of time is growing up and getting older —
> it's a universal thing so it's something most poets will write about.

Some poems explore the effects of Ageing on a Relationship

Sonnet 116 (Pages 4-5)

1) The poet says that true love <u>doesn't change</u>, even when people <u>get old</u> and lose their
"rosy lips and cheeks". He sees these physical attributes as <u>unimportant</u>.
2) He even says that true love can <u>survive</u> until "the edge of doom"
— the very last day at the <u>end of the world</u>.
3) He uses the <u>sonnet form</u>, which is often used for love poetry, to express his belief in <u>undying love</u>.

To His Coy Mistress (Pages 6-7)

1) The narrator makes <u>youth</u> seem like a <u>one-off opportunity</u> that <u>won't last long</u>
— "while the youthful hue / Sits on thy skin like morning dew".
2) He likens the process of ageing to being <u>chewed up</u> by time — "in his slow-chapt power".
3) He says they shouldn't <u>passively accept</u> this, but can <u>defy</u> the <u>ageing process</u> by grabbing
at life's pleasures with <u>youthful zest</u> — "tear our pleasures with rough strife."

People want to Protect Children as they Grow Up

Nettles (Pages 14-15)

1) The father <u>comforts</u> his very young son after he falls into some nettles.
2) Language connected with <u>war</u> is used as a metaphor for the damage the nettles
do, symbolising the pains of <u>growing up</u> — "that regiment of spite".
3) He likens life to a <u>battle</u>. He knows that as his son <u>grows up</u> although he tries to protect him,
he won't always be able to do so — "My son would often feel sharp wounds again".
4) This suggests that there is something <u>unavoidably painful</u> in the love a parent has for their child.

Born Yesterday (Pages 16-17)

1) Larkin wishes a <u>good</u> and <u>happy life</u> for newborn baby Sally.
2) He knows that <u>most people</u> will wish for Sally "the usual stuff / About being beautiful".
3) But he believes what will <u>really help</u> her to a "Catching of happiness" as she
grows up is "An average of talents", and this is what he wishes for Sally.
4) He uses the poem to show his <u>tenderness</u> towards his friend's
newborn daughter and his <u>genuine hope</u> for her future.

Other poems feature the theme of getting older...

'Sonnet 43' focuses on the narrator, rather than the other person in the relationship, growing
older. 'Brothers' describes a painful memory of growing up and failing to take responsibility.

Death

The spectre of death haunts many poems about relationships — it comes for us all in the end.

> 1) Death's an important theme as it marks the inevitable end of any relationship.
> 2) Some poets symbolise the power of their love by arguing that it'll last beyond death.

Death can be Difficult to Face

Harmonium (Pages 32-33)

1) Removing an old organ from the church makes the narrator's father talk about his own funeral.
2) The narrator feels awkward about this, and can't think of anything to say — "starved of breath".
3) The harmonium is old, with the "yellowed ...fingernails of its keys". His father, too, is old, "with smoker's fingers and dottled thumbs". Using similar imagery links the organ to his father and makes it seem like the father is also now past his best.
4) The last line is about silence, which might suggest that the narrator thinks they'll soon be unable to talk to each other any more.

To His Coy Mistress (Pages 6-7)

1) The narrator tries to use the idea of death to frighten his mistress into a more adventurous attitude to life, and into a sexual relationship with him — "The grave's a fine and private place, / But none, I think, do there embrace."
2) You could argue that he's also talking about his own horror at the thought of death — "And yonder all before us lie / Deserts of vast eternity."

Some poets write about Love carrying on beyond Death

Sonnet 116 (Pages 4-5)

1) The poet knows that life will eventually end — "Within his bending sickle's compass come".
2) He personifies time and says that all time gives us is "brief hours and weeks".
3) He acknowledges that life isn't always easy, and describes these difficulties as "tempests".
4) But he believes that true love will survive beyond the grave until the very last day of earth — "even to the edge of doom".

Sonnet 43 (Pages 10-11)

1) Lots of imagery — "soul", "Grace" and "Saints" — links her love to the idea of religion, which shows how deeply spiritual it is, and suggests that it may go beyond life and death.
2) She saves the last line of the poem to declare her belief that their love will not only survive beyond death but even get stronger — "I shall but love thee better after death".

Other poems feature the theme of betrayal and death...

'Sister Maude' is about the narrator's extreme reaction to the betrayal and death of her lover.

Memory

Memories of past events can inspire a whole range of emotions.

> 1) Painful memories can haunt people in later life.
> 2) Some memories can represent ongoing problems.

Memories can be Unpleasant to face

The Manhunt (Pages 18-19)

1) The soldier has returned from the war but finds it difficult to <u>come to terms</u> with what he has been through, and has "<u>buried</u>" the experience "<u>deep in his mind</u>".
2) He is <u>unable</u> or <u>unwilling</u> to think <u>too deeply</u> about what happened to him — "every nerve in his body had tightened and closed".
3) The poem may also have a <u>more general message</u> about the <u>effects of war</u> on individuals as they try to live with <u>traumatic memories</u>.

He's smiling blankly in the hope you won't notice he's completely forgotten who you are.

Brothers (Pages 28-29)

1) The narrator looks back on the memory of leaving his brother behind with <u>regret</u>.
2) He <u>blames himself</u> for it — and finds it difficult to <u>come to terms</u> with the memory of his <u>neglect</u>, even though it happened so long ago.
3) The memory of this event seems to have been the source of a "<u>distance</u>" in their relationship.

The Farmer's Bride (Pages 8-9)

1) The farmer <u>remembers</u> when, "Three Summers" ago, he chose his young bride.
2) But after they married she <u>changed</u> and "<u>her smile went out</u>".
3) He recalls how she <u>ran away</u> from him and had to be "chased" and how he "fetched her home".
4) Most of the poem takes the form of the narrator describing events from the past and he does so with a <u>regretful</u> but <u>gentle tone</u> — it's only in the last stanza that the tone shifts to one of desperation.
5) This suggests that <u>bad memories</u> continue to <u>hurt</u>, and <u>add tension</u> to people's lives in the present.

Painful Memories never go away

Nettles (Pages 14-15)

1) The poet remembers when his very young son was <u>hurt</u>.
2) He recalls his <u>anger</u> at the nettles for causing his son to <u>suffer</u>.
3) He attempted to punish the nettles by cutting them down — "<u>slashed in fury</u>" — and then burning them on a "<u>funeral pyre</u>".
4) But he remembers how <u>quickly</u> they grew back "in two weeks" — the memory seems to stick with him as it was the <u>first time</u> he realised he couldn't <u>protect his son completely</u>.

Other poems feature the theme of memory...

'Sonnet 43' suggests that a relationship can draw up feelings from the narrator's childhood.
'Praise Song For My Mother' features the narrator's happy memories of her mother.

Nature

Poets often use images of nature to describe their feelings.

> 1) Natural imagery suggests that something is beautiful and unspoilt.
> 2) Nature can also be used to suggest that something is wild or dangerous.

Natural images can be Positive

Ghazal (Pages 26-27)

1) The poem includes imagery of gardens — "grass", "rose", "laurel leaf", "bark", "leaf"
— these show that her love is as natural and beautiful as a garden of paradise.
2) She also includes animals — "bird", "serpent", "hawk", "moth" —
these present her love as a living, breathing thing.
3) She believes her lover can create paradise on earth for her — "Be heaven and earth to me".

Praise Song For My Mother (Pages 30-31)

1) The poet uses imagery connected with the essential elements of life — "water", "sunrise".
She also uses food from her home country — "fish's red gill", "crab's leg", "fried plantain".
2) She admires her mother as a constant giver of life — "replenishing replenishing".
3) She uses the imagery of the natural force of the moon pulling the tide to show how she
was drawn to her mother's all-embracing love — "You were / moon's eye to me / pull".

Sometimes images of Nature can be Sinister

My love for you is
like a marmot.

The Farmer's Bride (Pages 8-9)

1) The unhappy bride is frequently compared to small animals —
"like a hare", "like a mouse", "shy as a leveret".
2) All of these are prey animals, which suggest she's constantly
watching out for predators.
3) Like a wild animal, when she felt cornered "she runned away".

Nettles (Pages 14-15)

1) The nettles are presented with imagery of battle — they're described as a "fierce parade".
2) They are a source of pain for the poet's young son — "With sobs and tears".
3) Their power to harm is explored and made into a metaphor for the
pains of life — "My son would often feel sharp wounds again."
4) After the father chops down the nettles they soon grow back — "the busy sun and rain / Had called
up tall recruits". This could suggest that suffering is part of nature and the natural order of things.

There are other poems that refer to nature...

'Sonnet 116' compares life to a voyage on the ocean and love to a star, which are both natural
images. In 'To His Coy Mistress' the narrator suggests that he and his mistress act like birds of prey.

Pain and Desire

Relationships rarely go exactly as we want them to.

> 1) Even the closest relationships — whether in families, friends or couples — involve tensions and disagreements.
> 2) Before romantic relationships get going there is often a period of frustrated desire.

Characters in poems sometimes feel Hurt

Quickdraw (Pages 24-25)

1) The narrator is so desperately waiting for a telephone call from her lover that she is carrying her phones around with her — "I wear the two ... / slung from the pockets on my hips".
2) When she gets the call though, it upsets her as if she has been shot "through the heart".
3) She uses the imagery of the old film and TV Westerns to express how painful love can be. Even the texted kisses of her lover hit her like bullets — "Take this ... / and this ..."

Harmonium (Pages 32-33)

1) The narrator is unhappy when his father makes a bad joke about the instrument being carried out of the church — "the next box... will bear the freight of his own dead weight".
2) He seems to be wearied by his father's talk about death — "And he, being him, can't help but say".
3) It seems to hurt him more to think about his father's death than it bothers his father.
4) He doesn't know how to answer his father's comments — he can only "mouth in reply / some shallow or sorry phrase or word".

Some characters are motivated by Desire

In Paris With You (Pages 22-23)

1) The character feels that he has been messed around by his previous lover — "I'm angry at the way I've been bamboozled".
2) But by the end of the poem his focus has shifted onto his physical desire for his potential lover — "I'm in Paris with your eyes, your mouth".
3) You could argue that desire for this other person has dragged him out of his self-absorbed misery.

To His Coy Mistress (Pages 6-7)

1) The narrator makes no attempt to disguise the fact that he's motivated by physical desire.
2) He suggests that while she may not have welcomed his lust, the chance to enjoy it will soon be gone, when he or she dies — "And your quaint honour turn to dust, / And into ashes all my lust."
3) His desire is clear by the effort that he puts into trying to persuade her, and in the passionate, violent imagery he uses in the last stanza — "like amorous birds of prey".
4) He seems to be suggesting that by putting their passion into practice they will be able to live more intensely and powerfully — "through the iron gates of life."

Other poems feature pain and desire...

In 'The Farmer's Bride' the farmer is clearly pained by his wife's rejection of him, and still feels a strong desire for her. 'Hour' is a poem that unites the more romantic images of love with those of an earthy desire and an afternoon spent in a grass ditch.

Forms of Poetry

I've chosen to write this poem in the form of a revision guide.

> 1) The writers whose work is in this anthology have chosen to express their ideas in poetic form.
> 2) This gives them freedom from some of the rules of other forms of writing, such as grammar, punctuation and paragraphing.
> 3) But poetic forms often have their own "rules" about how they're made up.

Some Poetic Forms follow a very Strict Pattern

Sonnet 116 (Pages 4-5) and Sonnet 43 (Pages 10-11)

1) The sonnet is a poetic form which has been written for hundreds of years. It's usually used to express love, and that's what Shakespeare and Barrett Browning have done.
2) A sonnet has 14 lines which are usually written in iambic pentameter.
3) Shakespearean sonnets have three sets of four lines (quatrains) which rhyme in an ABAB pattern with a rhyming couplet at the end.
4) Barrett Browning's sonnet follows a different sonnet structure, called the Petrarchan form. It has a group of eight lines followed by a set of six lines, rhyming ABBAABBA CDCDCD.
5) Writing to such strict rules keeps the ideas really focused. Every word has to be carefully chosen and placed within the constraints of the 14 lines, within the rhythmic structure and the rhyme scheme.

Other Forms have Rules about Content

Ghazal (Pages 26-27)

1) This poetic form is often about the pain of being apart from a loved one.
2) The couplets are supposed to be unconnected, so that each one could be read on its own, or removed without destroying the poem. This means that there can't be enjambment between stanzas.
3) This poem makes use of the form to present us with a dizzying series of images showing different aspects of love.

Some Poems have a much Less Strict Pattern

Quickdraw (Pages 24-25)

1) The narrator doesn't know when the phone will ring and the uneven structure reflects the uncertainty about when the calls will come and also what will be said — things she wants to hear and things she doesn't.
2) The uneven structure, with some split lines, reflects this uncertainty.
3) It's as if she can't control the lines of the poem in the same way she can't control the timing and content of the telephone calls.

Harmonium (Pages 32-33)

1) The narrator is remembering a particular time with his father.
2) He structures the poem into stanzas showing different moments from the memory.
3) But there is not much of a rhythm or rhyme scheme — as though he is working his way through the memory and exploring the feelings he had at the time.

You could talk about form with any poem...

Some poems play around with form. 'Hour' starts out like a Shakespearean sonnet, discussing time and love in personified terms, but stretches the form by using different line lengths.

Poetic Devices

Poetic devices are all those little tricks poets use to liven up their writing. The crazy cats.

1) You need to be able to identify different techniques used in the poems and make comparisons between them.
2) It's really important that you don't just say what the technique is, but include details of what effect it has on the poem.

Strawberry's my favourite flavour of enjambment.

Poetic Devices include Enjambment...

To His Coy Mistress (Pages 6-7)

1) The enjambment makes his thoughts seem spontaneous — "Thou by the Indian Ganges' side / Shouldst rubies find; I by the tide / Of Humber would complain..."
2) It's as though he is thinking on the spot of all the things he can to persuade his mistress.

Hour (Pages 20-21)

1) The poet is recalling a precious hour of love when time seemed to stand still.
2) The enjambment slows the poem down to reflect this
   — "Time slows, for here / we are millionaires".

...Layout...

Quickdraw (Pages 24-25)

1) The narrator doesn't know when the telephone call will come.
   When the phone does suddenly ring, the call is painful.
2) Indenting "You've wounded me" and "through the heart" emphasises the pain the character feels.

Praise Song For My Mother (Pages 30-31)

1) The mother's love is generous and gives emotional nourishment to her child.
2) Offsetting the repeated word "replenishing" stresses this most important message which sums up the narrator's overwhelmingly positive view of her mother.

...and Repetition

The Manhunt (Pages 18-19)

1) Importance is given to the repeated phrase "only then" — it emphasises the fact that she's taking small steps and making slow progress.
2) This suggests that it takes time, love and patience for the narrator to reach an understanding of her husband's mental state and for him to begin to allow her to see his anguish.

You can find poetic devices in most poems...

'Praise Song For My Mother' uses repetition of "You were..." to emphasise the different aspects of her relationship with her mother. 'Brothers' uses enjambment in a way that gives it a conversational, anecdotal tone. The song-like ballad 'Sister Maude' uses more end-stopped lines.

Beginnings of Poems

The beginning's as good a place to start as any.

> 1) The beginning of any poem is really important as it sets out what the poem is going to be about.
> 2) It also can set the tone for a poem — if it's going to be angry, happy, bitter, etc...
> 3) The opening of a poem sets up expectations of what the rest of the poem is going to be like — the poet can either fulfil or challenge these expectations.

Beginnings can be used to Set the Scene

Nettles (Pages 14-15)

1) The first line gives a straightforward opening, clearly telling the reader what the poem is going to be about.
2) However, from the very next line the poem begins to explore metaphorical images — looking at the idea of a nettle "bed" and introducing the battle metaphor which is extended throughout the poem — "spears".

Beginnings can also Set the Tone

Sister Maude (Pages 12-13)

1) The first stanza lets the reader understand how bitter the sister is about Maude.
2) She uses rhetorical questions to show that she knows exactly who told her parents about the secret relationship she was having — "Who told my father of my dear?"
3) By the end of the first stanza we are in no doubt about how she views Maude's actions — "Who lurked to spy and peer".

Born Yesterday (Pages 16-17)

1) The narrator makes it clear from the outset that his wish for Sally is going to be different from those of other people.
2) He begins with an image of the baby as a "Tightly-folded bud". This has an almost literal meaning, as newborn babies are often crumpled in on themselves, still curled up in the fetal position.
3) The first lines suggest that he is going to wish the baby something special — "something / None of the others would". This expectation seems to be dashed when he goes on to wish her not to be attractive or too talented.

In Paris With You (Pages 22-23)

1) A sense of hurt and bitterness is conveyed in the very first line — "Don't talk to me of love."
2) The colloquial language ("I've had an earful") is continued throughout the poem, giving it an ironic tone.

You could talk about the beginning of any poem...

'The Manhunt' starts out with what could be the opening lines of a standard love poem, and only later establishes the theme of dealing with the trauma of war. 'Hour' begins in a quite similar way to 'Sonnet 116', but then takes on a more intimate tone.

Couplets and Last Lines

Writers often try to make their poems go out with a bang.

> 1) The last lines of poems often leave the reader with a powerful image or idea.
> 2) They can also be used to provide a twist — something unexpected.

Closing Couplets and Last Lines can Sum Up a Poem

Sonnet 116 (Pages 4-5)

1) The last two lines of a Shakespearean sonnet rhyme.
2) In this sonnet, the narrator says that everything he's said about love in the poem is true.
3) He says that if it isn't true, then he never wrote anything, and no man has ever been in love.
4) He's challenging the reader to disagree with him — which makes him sound completely convinced of the truth of his own words.

Praise Song For My Mother (Pages 30-31)

1) The last line is on its own, making it stand out from the rest of the poem.
2) It sums up her mother's giving nature, in encouraging her child to leave and discover her own destiny.
3) The last lines also suggest a fond farewell, and the end of the stage in the narrator's life when the narrator was reliant on her mother.

"My poem won't have a last line. That'll learn 'em."

Closing Lines can be Surprising

The Farmer's Bride (Pages 8 9)

1) The farmer has told the story of his young bride and her aversion to him, "she turned afraid / Of love and me".
2) We know that she now sleeps apart from him, "She sleeps up in the attic there / Alone".
3) The final lines are passionate, as he thinks of her with her soft skin, her brown hair and eyes.
4) There's also a troubled mood to the end of the poem — even though he feels sympathy for her, "poor maid", we get the sense he is struggling to control his desires. The poem concludes on an uncertain note with a sense of threat.

Brothers (Pages 28-29)

1) The poem's last line leaves the reader with the sense that something bigger was taking place, not just the simple action of children running for a bus.
2) He feels that at the time he was powerless to stop himself — "I ran on, unable to close the distance".
3) The poem ends with the narrator looking back to his younger brother — it also suggests the idea of the poet looking back on his own past. This gives the poem a melancholy and reflective ending.

These other poems have interesting endings...

'Nettles' ends with the sad conclusion that painful events would often be repeated afterwards and can't be prevented. 'Born Yesterday' uses a final rhyming couplet to give a powerful, heartfelt ending to quite a conversational and ironic poem.

Rhyme and Rhythm

Rhyme and rhythm are what make poetry poetry.

> 1) Poets can use rhyme to emphasise thoughts and emotions — and give them a sense of order and completeness that they may lack in prose sentences.
>
> 2) Poets can use rhythm to help fix their words in the reader's memory — just like a catchy tune.

Rhyme can add Force to the poet's message

Ghazal (Pages 26-27)

1) The rhyming words before the repeated "me" at the end of stanzas add urgency to the plea for the lover to respond to her passion — "then woo me ... tattoo me ... bedew me ... pursue me ... renew me".
2) The repeated rhymes add to a sense of expectation as we want to know how each stanza is going to fit in with the rhyme.

Born Yesterday (Pages 16-17)

1) This is a largely unrhymed poem, but it ends with a rhyming couplet.
2) This emphasises the contrast between the more conversational start with its ironic tone, and the message which the final couplet delivers — which is sincere and deeply felt.

The Rhythm can make things Stand Out

Sister Maude (Pages 12-13)

1) The regular rhythm of the first stanza pushes the embittered words out, emphasising the anger and hatred of the sister as she asks her rhetorical questions — "Who told my mother of my shame?"
2) The poem is made up of short words which keeps up the pace of the poem, and adds emphasis to the rhythm, e.g. "Bide *you* with death and sin." This helps give the poem its intensely angry tone.

Praise Song For My Mother (Pages 30-31)

1) The fourth stanza is longer than the others and has longer lines. This allows the definitions to become more detailed and precise.
2) The rhythm changes in the final line to reflect the change in the narrative — the mother has given her child all she can during her upbringing and knows she is now ready to explore her own destiny — "Go to your wide futures, you said".

The Farmer's Bride (Pages 8-9)

1) The poem has a fairly regular rhythm as the farmer calmly describes the unhappy events that have taken place. But at some points the rhythm changes, suggesting the presence of strong emotions.
2) In the second stanza, we learn of the bride's escape and recapture. The faster rhythm reflects her panicked flight across the fields — "We chased her, flying like a hare".
3) The breakdown of the rhythm at the end gives a sense of the farmer's battle with his desire for his young bride. It's almost as though he can no longer contain the words in a rhythmic pattern in the same way that he can no longer contain his passion — "Oh! my God! the down... her hair, her hair!"

These other poems use rhyme and rhythm...

'Quickdraw' use internal rhymes, which emphasise the looser, more unpredictable structure.
'In Paris With You' uses humorous, unexpected and contrived rhymes, giving it a slightly ironic tone.

Use of First Person

Writing in the first person can express personal feelings. I like writing in the first person.

> 1) A poem written in the first person is one where the narrator is a character in the poem — it'll use words like "I" and "me".
> 2) Other poems are written in the third person — e.g. "She rode her bicycle."
> 3) Writing in the first person gives the poet a chance to describe the world from their own or a character's point of view.

Writing in the First Person can express Personal Feelings

The Manhunt (Pages 18-19)

1) The wife of the injured soldier <u>explores</u> her husband's injuries.
2) The use of the <u>first person</u> means we go through the process with her — "only then could I picture the scan."
3) Using the first person means that the <u>tone</u> of the poem directly relates to the <u>emotions</u> of the narrator. She sounds <u>calm</u> and <u>measured</u>, suggesting the careful approach she has had to take, in contrast to the <u>tension</u> and <u>trauma</u> that her husband is going through.

Hour (Pages 20-21)

1) The narrator uses <u>first person</u> to show how delighted she is in the <u>physical</u> love she enjoys — "we kiss".
2) The poem starts out in the <u>third person</u>, talking about love and time in general. This adds <u>emphasis</u> to the moment where it shifts to the narrator's own <u>experience</u> — "We find an hour together...".
3) Putting the narrative into the <u>first person</u> means the reader gets a sense of <u>sharing</u> in the experience, rather than just <u>witnessing</u> it.

It can add Impact to the Poem

Ghazal (Pages 26-27)

1) The writer <u>explores</u> her relationship with her lover by constantly repeating "If I...and you".
2) This simple, direct address emphasises the <u>deep feelings</u> of love which the poet reveals.

Brothers (Pages 28-29)

1) The <u>guilt</u> that the narrator feels at having run off and left his six-year-old sibling is <u>shared</u> directly with the reader, even though he actually talks to the youngster — "while you skipped..."
2) He reveals his feelings of <u>frustration</u> directly — "I sighed".

In Paris With You (Pages 22-23)

1) The narrator continually refers to <u>himself</u> — "I've had an earful", "I get tearful", "I'm one of your...", "I'm angry".
2) This reveals he is <u>self-absorbed</u> at the start of the poem — "I'm a hostage. I'm marooned."
3) Putting the poem in the <u>first person</u> means that it's as if we're the ones being addressed. Rather than just being a story, we're made to <u>feel</u> as if <u>we are there</u>.

He'd quit poetry to concentrate on becoming the first person.

These other poems are in the first person...

...in fact they all are. 'Sonnet 116' uses it as a personal guarantee of what seem more general reflections about love. Putting the narrative in the first person gives 'The Farmer's Bride' an added tension as we get a portrait of the farmer's state of mind as well as a description of the events.

Imagery

Imagery is like a crazy lion eating an ice cream.

1) Imagery can give the reader a sense of physical, sensory experience.
2) Poets use imagery in metaphors and similes to make poems more descriptive.

"We'd like more poems with fishing imagery."

Some poets translate Time into Imagery

Sonnet 116 (Pages 4-5)

1) Shakespeare uses a traditional personification of time — an old man with a "sickle" to harvest corn. This links time with ideas of death.
2) This imagery helps to support his representation of true love as being able to transcend time — "Love's not Time's fool".
3) This poem also uses seafaring imagery. This makes the poem a more sensuous experience than just writing out its message. It suggests that love guides us in an uncertain and dangerous world.
4) We experience a sense of danger through the word "tempests". Love's eternal nature and independence from the world is emphasised when it's compared to a star.

Poets use a lot of Natural Imagery

Ghazal (Pages 26-27)

1) This compares the narrator and her lover to plants and animals to explore their relationship.
2) The poet uses these images to play with ideas of power within the relationship. Sometimes she makes herself seem subservient — "I am the laurel leaf in your crown" — and sometimes more dangerous — "If mine is the venomous tongue, the serpent's tail".
3) Using natural images allows her to suggest that there is a darker side to love, without making that seem unnatural. She wants him to be "hawk to my shadow" but also "moth to my flame" — this suggests an animal-like, instinctive attraction, but also a powerful, dangerous one.

Nettles (Pages 14-15)

1) The poet personifies the bed of nettles as an army. This becomes an extended metaphor through the poem comparing this accident to an act of war — "spears", "recruits".
2) This helps the poet bring out the deep significance in an otherwise everyday occurrence. It helps show how he was moved by the kind of accident that happens to every child growing up.

Praise Song For My Mother (Pages 30-31)

1) Imagery of nature in "water", the "sunrise", "moon" and food demonstrate the mother's all-providing love for her children.
2) The choice of food imagery also ties this in to a particular place and time.
3) The overall effect is to show how the mother stood at the centre of the narrator's world.
4) There are lots of different possible interpretations — for example, the first stanza could suggest the power of the sea or the way water cleanses us. This means the poem explores what the mother's love was to the narrator — it doesn't define or limit it.

There's plenty of imagery in these poems...

'To His Coy Mistress' also uses imagery connected with time, but for very different ends than 'Sonnet 116'. 'The Farmer's Bride' uses a lot of nature imagery, which gives us a picture of the kind of person the farmer is, as well as making his bride seem like a frightened wild animal.

Unusual Vocabulary

This page is all about the weird and wacky words of poets. Ka-boom.

> 1) Poems are a way of using language in a concentrated way.
> Every aspect of the words contributes to the meaning.
> 2) Sometimes poets will use language in deliberately unusual ways to get the reader
> to notice something that might be missed if it was expressed more conventionally.

Strange Words force the reader to take Another Look

Quickdraw (Pages 24-25)

1) The repetition of the final words "take this" continues the theme
of a gunfight in an old Western film or TV show.
2) These words are likened to bullets fired out of a gun — this sums up the connections
between modern communications and Old West imagery in the poem.

Harmonium (Pages 32-33)

1) The poet suggests the music of the harmonium by using alliteration
in "its hummed harmonics... for a hundred years".
2) The third stanza of the poem is about the harmony between fathers and sons over the
generations as they sang in the choir, to the accompaniment of the organ — "had
opened their throats / and gilded finches – like high notes – had streamed out."
3) This strange image stands out against the mostly normal,
down-to-earth language of the rest of the poem.

Vocabulary can help describe Characters

The Farmer's Bride (Pages 8-9)

1) The dialect of the farmer is made clear in the words he uses —
"'twasn't a woman", "'Tis but a stair / Betwixt us".
2) It allows him to talk directly to us. This perhaps makes us feel sympathy for
him, as it makes us realise that he didn't mean to scare his young bride.

Praise Song For My Mother (Pages 30-31)

1) Nichols uses an unusually compact method of communicating her ideas. She uses a number of
carefully chosen words to explain what her mother was to her, e.g. "You were / sunrise to me".
2) The poem also contains many words that don't seem to have a simple meaning —
"fathoming" suggests both a great depth and great understanding, "mantling" suggests
covering and protecting, and "streaming" suggests a constant pouring in like light.
3) The complex language means that this is a poem which wants its meaning
to be explored and extended and won't have a simple final meaning.
Like the mother's love, this poem is beyond a simple description.

You can find unusual vocabulary in other poems too...

'To His Coy Mistress' contains such odd turns of phrase as "vegetable love". When you notice
something odd in these poems, have a good think about why the poet might have used those words.

Irony and Sarcasm

Why can't they just say what they mean?

> 1) Irony is when you say one thing and mean another. It's often used in a comic way, but also can have a more serious meaning.
>
> 2) Sarcasm is like irony, but has a cruel twist to it. It comes from Ancient Greek, and literally means "flesh-tearing".

Irony can express Painful Memories

Nettles (Pages 14-15)

1) The poet considers the irony in the term "nettle bed".
2) He calls it a "curious name" for them, and says that "It was no place for rest."
3) A bed for a small child should be safe and comfortable — the raw pain which the nettles caused his son makes this particular word seem inappropriate for these weeds.

Brothers (Pages 28-29)

1) This poem is about the tension between what the young brothers thought they knew, and what the narrator knows about his youth in hindsight.
2) The two elder brothers think they're mature, but ironically this just makes it clearer that they're children — "I was nine and he was ten / and we must stroll the town, doing what grown-ups do."

Poets use Sarcasm to Make a Point

To His Coy Mistress (Pages 6-7)

1) The narrator uses hyperbole to exaggerate how much time he'd like to spend courting his mistress — "An hundred years should go to praise / Thine eyes". He's sarcastically mocking traditional ideas of courtship. He sees the delay as a waste of time.
2) He also uses sarcasm to frighten his mistress with the thought of death — "The grave's a fine and private place, / But none, I think, do there embrace."

Born Yesterday (Pages 16-17)

1) Larkin writes ironically about "the usual stuff" which people sentimentally wish for a child.
2) He sarcastically describes the usual wishes that she should end up "running off a spring / Of innocence and love" — this sounds scornful and dismissive.
3) He doubts that it's possible to live up to such an ideal. He points out that these are a matter of chance — "Well, you're a lucky girl". His sarcasm makes these ideals seem unrealistic.
4) He wants her to be happy, and the sarcasm shows how little he rates the traditional ideal as a way of achieving it.

These poems also contain irony and sarcasm...

'In Paris With You' is set in the romantic city of Paris, but has many elements that seem the opposite of romantic, and it mixes the misery of the narrator with humorous rhymes. 'Harmonium' describes the damage done to the harmonium, but it's the narrator whose words are "starved of breath".

Mood

Mood is the general feel and emotion of the poem. Not what the cow did.

"Poems always put me in a mood."

1) Poets establish a mood with their choice of vocabulary, in how they describe the setting, adjectives, adverbs, etc.
2) The situation and events of the poem also contribute to the mood.

Some poets create an Unhappy Mood

The Farmer's Bride (Pages 8-9)

1) The poem takes us through the seasons but we are left with a bitterly cold winter scene — "the black earth spread white with rime." Winter imagery is often used to convey unhappiness.
2) This contrasts with the spring imagery the narrator uses to describe his wife — "Sweet as the first wild violets". Spring suggests new life and hope, but that's all in the past now.
3) There is also an uneasy mood to the poem as we get the sense that he is struggling to control his passion for her, which is shown by the repetition of words as he thinks about her physical presence — "the down, / The soft young down of her..."

Harmonium (Pages 32-33)

1) A melancholy mood is established in this poem with the mix of precise details and gentle humour describing the sad image of the old harmonium, no longer used by the church.
2) Mixing details of the present with his imagining of the past creates a reflective mood — "holes were worn in both the treadles / where the organist's feet... had pedalled and pedalled."
3) The mood shifts in the last stanza as the focus goes from the harmonium onto the narrator's father. The joke his father makes leaves him speechless. This means the poem ends with a sadder, more sombre mood.

Mood can be shown in Different Ways

In Paris With You (Pages 22-23)

1) The writer is clearly upset about a previous, failed relationship — "Don't talk to me of love...I get tearful". So there is a bitter note in the poem's mood.
2) The mood is made complex by the setting which is both romantic — Paris — and also unromantic — a sleazy hotel. This uncertain mood is added to by the narrator's lack of interest in "where are we bound", which contrasts with his close attention to his lover — "I'm in Paris with the slightest thing you do."

Sonnet 43 (Pages 10-11)

1) The poet uses repetition and religious language to build up an intense and passionate mood — "I love thee purely".
2) The poet uses an outburst of short words to describe how her love extends through her life — "I love thee with the breath, / Smiles, tears, of all my life!" This gives the poem a more emotional and less controlled mood.

Think about the mood of all these poems...

'To His Coy Mistress' is both passionate and witty. 'Sister Maude' uses alliteration and repetition to convey a very angry mood. The loose rhythm of 'Hour' gives it quite a relaxed, romantic mood.

The Poetry Exam: Unit Two Overview

If you're following <u>Route A</u> of the AQA English Literature course, you'll have to do
an <u>exam</u> called <u>Unit 2: Poetry Across Time</u>. That's what this page is all about.

Your Exam <u>Will be</u> Split Up <u>Like This</u>

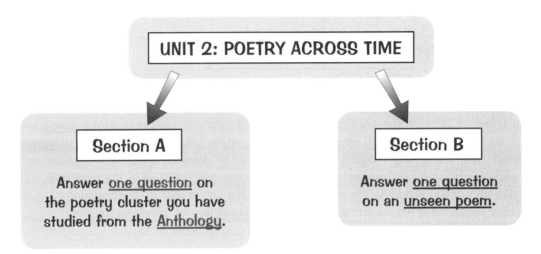

1) This guide contains all the poems from the '<u>Relationships</u>' cluster of the Anthology — this should be the one you've studied in class. There are three other poetry clusters, which you <u>don't</u> need to <u>worry about</u>.

2) The next few pages will give you <u>tips</u> on how to answer the question in <u>Section A</u>.

3) Section A is worth <u>two-thirds</u> of the marks in the <u>exam</u> and nearly a <u>quarter</u> of your entire <u>GCSE</u>.

This is How <u>Your Exam</u> <u>Will Work</u>

1) The whole exam lasts <u>1 hour 15 minutes</u>. You should spend about <u>45 minutes</u> on <u>Section A</u>. The other 30 minutes should be spent doing Section B.

2) Section A has a <u>choice</u> of <u>two questions</u> for each poetry cluster. You should only answer <u>one question</u> and it should be about the cluster you've <u>studied</u>. The question is worth <u>36 marks</u>.

3) You're <u>not allowed</u> to take your <u>own anthology</u> or any <u>notes</u> about the poems into the exam. You'll be given a <u>blank copy</u> of the anthology to help you with your answer.

4) You'll also be given a <u>separate answer book</u> to write your answer in.

There are <u>Instructions</u> <u>on the</u> Front Page <u>of the</u> Exam

1) You <u>must read</u> the <u>front page</u> of the exam paper <u>before</u> you start — it tells you <u>exactly</u> what to do.

2) There will be a <u>list</u> of things you need for the exam. Make sure you've got <u>everything</u> on it.

3) Check you've got the <u>right exam paper</u> — it should be the one for the <u>higher tier</u>.

4) Remember to fill in <u>all the details</u> on the front page of the <u>answer booklet</u>.

<u>I hope you're paying attention — there's an exam on this...</u>
I like pages like this. Absolutely <u>no learning</u> whatsoever. Lovely. Don't worry if you forget some of this stuff — there'll be a <u>reminder</u> of how the exam works on the <u>front page</u> of the exam paper.

Sample Question 1

OK, so now you know what the <u>exam's about</u>. I bet you're just <u>dying</u> to find out what the questions will be like, eh? Er, well... Here's your <u>first sample question</u> anyway.

Read the Question Carefully and Underline Key Words

1) You'll have a <u>choice</u> of <u>two questions</u>, so it's best to <u>read</u> them both through <u>carefully</u> first. Then pick the one you think you've got the <u>best chance</u> of answering well.

2) Once you've done that, <u>read</u> the question you've chosen through <u>again</u>. <u>Underline</u> the question's <u>theme</u> and any other important words.

3) The question will give you the title of <u>one poem</u> and ask you to <u>compare</u> it to <u>one other</u> poem of <u>your choice</u>. Pick another poem you think relates to the theme.

4) <u>Look up</u> the poems you're going to write about in the <u>blank copy</u> of the <u>anthology</u> you'll be given in the exam. <u>Turn over the corners</u> of the pages they're on so you can find them again <u>quickly</u>.

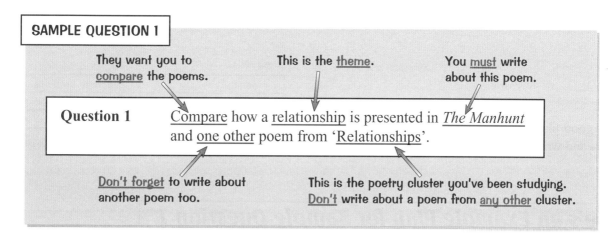

SAMPLE QUESTION 1

They want you to <u>compare</u> the poems.

This is the <u>theme</u>.

You <u>must</u> write about this poem.

Question 1   Compare how a <u>relationship</u> is presented in *The Manhunt* and <u>one other</u> poem from 'Relationships'.

<u>Don't forget</u> to write about another poem too.

This is the poetry cluster you've been studying. <u>Don't</u> write about a poem from <u>any other</u> cluster.

There are Three Main Ways to Get Marks

<u>Whichever</u> question you choose to answer, you'll get marks for:

(1) Giving your own <u>thoughts</u> and <u>opinions</u> on the poems and supporting them with <u>quotes</u> from the text.

(2) <u>Explaining</u> features like <u>form</u>, <u>structure</u> and <u>language</u>.

(3) Describing the <u>similarities</u> and <u>differences</u> between poems.

In 18th century Scotland, the penalty for forgetting to include quotes was severe.

Keep these <u>three things</u> in mind when you're <u>writing</u> and <u>planning</u> your answer.

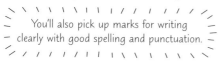
You'll also pick up marks for writing clearly with good spelling and punctuation.

Read the question carefully...

If only I'd always followed that particular <u>piece of advice</u> myself — there might never have been that <u>unfortunate incident</u> with the policeman and the chocolate orange. Still, we live and learn.

Planning

If you were to ask me what my best tip would be for getting great marks in your exam, I would not say "bribe the examiner". Oh no. That would be wrong. I'd say "plan your essay answers".

Spend Five Minutes Planning Your Answer

1) Always plan your answer before you start — that way, you're less likely to forget something important.

2) Write your plan at the top of your answer booklet and draw a neat line through it when you've finished.

3) Don't spend too long on your plan. It's only rough work, so you don't need to write in full sentences. Here are a few examples of different ways you can plan your answer:

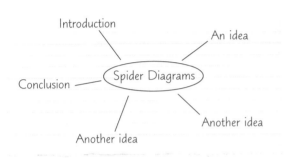

Spider Diagrams

- Introduction
- An idea
- Conclusion
- Another idea
- Another idea

Bullet points with...
- Intro...
- An idea...
- The next idea...

Tables with...

A point...	Quote to back this up...
Another point...	Quote...
A different point...	Quote...
A brand new point...	Quote...

4) A good plan will help you organise your ideas — and write a good, well-structured essay.

Here's an Example Plan for Sample Question 1

Here's a possible plan for Sample Question 1. When you're writing your plan, remember to keep in mind the three main ways to get marks from p.55. And keep it brief.

Plan: poem 1 = The Manhunt, poem 2 = Nettles

1) Introduction — kind of relationships in each poem
- Poem 1 — wife — passion, love, fear for husband's condition, compassion
- Poem 2 — love and compassion too

2) Language Comparison
- Poem 1 — unusual imagery (soldier as delicate) — 'porcelain', 'parachute silk' link to mental state
- Poem 2 — unusual imagery — again, war and battle — dad's need to protect son

3) Form and Structure Comparison
- Poem 1 — rhyming couplets — cheerful, simple rhyme contrasts with serious subject
- Poem 2 — simple rhyme scheme, serious subject

4) Wider Issues — why poem was written
- Poem 1 — explores wife's feelings for husband / effects of war on individuals
- Poem 2 — explores parent's feelings for child

5) Summary — Comparing — 'Both these poems...'

> Use your plan to start making links between the poems.

> Jot down any good quotes you want to use.

> Don't forget to write about language, form and structure.

> Write about ideas and attitudes too.

You can't write a great essay without a good plan...

This is time well spent — five minutes spent planning your answer in an exam will help you get a much better mark. Practise by planning your own answers to the sample questions in this guide.

THIS IS A FLAP.
FOLD THIS PAGE OUT.

How to Answer the Question

Both poets react physically to the injuries of their loved one. Scannell uses aggression, conveyed by the violent language "slashed... till not a nettle... Stood", while Armitage's narrator Laura more cautiously "traced the scarring". While Scannell vents his anger at his son's accident in destructive physical activity, "I took my hook... and slashed in fury", Laura's voice is patient and gentle: "only then could I". Through both poets' choice of words, we too can feel not only the physical pain of the victims, but the anguish of both father and wife at witnessing the injuries, the "white blisters beaded" on the small boy and the "fractured rudder of shoulder-blade" of the man. At this point, both realise that the best they can offer is comfort.

It's a good idea to judge the poems side-by-side.

Laura's love seems to have no time limit. Repetition of the phrase "only then" suggests that Laura believes that her patient, supportive love may heal her husband's mental and physical scars, even though it may take a long time. Scannell, on the other hand, sees with anguish that his love cannot protect his son for ever. Despite all of his attempts to get rid of the nettles, he knows that his efforts are only limited in their effectiveness; it only takes "two weeks" of the "busy sun and rain" for them to grow back. Although Scannell conveys helplessness against events and the passage of time, Armitage carries a message of hope, that time is immaterial to love.

Write about differences between the poems too.

Try to work quotes into your sentences when you can.

By exploring the wife's loving protection of her husband and her desire to "feel" his hurt and "come close" to understanding his injuries so that she can help him come to terms with them, Armitage leaves the reader with a possibly political message about the impact of war on individuals and their relationships with each other. It is a message that seems especially relevant today with the ongoing debates about the wars in Iraq and Afghanistan. Scannell however makes a more universal point when he presents the reader with his view on how helpless all parents are when it comes to being able to protect their children from the pains of life.

You can consider why the poem's been written.

Include your personal response to the poems.

Both of these poems present strong, loving relationships. The soldier's wife and the young boy's father feel a sense of protectiveness over the other person in the relationship. They both want to try to help by comforting and are anxious to take care of them to prevent any further harm or damage. Laura believes that, with time and patience, this may be possible while the father in 'Nettles' seems to take a more pessimistic view about his power to help his son.

It's good to end with a clear summary of your ideas.

Wider Issues

Conclusion

How to Answer the Question

Here's an 'A' grade sample answer to the exam question on p.55.

Compare how a relationship is presented in The Manhunt
and one other poem from 'Relationships'.

1 Introduction

Relationships are the connections between people. In 'The Manhunt', Simon Armitage explores the relationship between a wife and her husband, an injured soldier who has returned from battle. In 'Nettles', the relationship is between a father and his young son who has fallen into a bed of stinging nettles. Both poets explore the compassion felt by the narrator of the poem for the other person in the relationship. In 'The Manhunt', the narrator's compassion is for the mental anguish which her husband is obviously suffering and in 'Nettles' it is the father's compassion for the physical wounds of his son.

It can be a good idea to briefly define key terms in the question.

Tell the examiner how both poems relate to the theme.

2 Language

Both poets use unusual imagery to present the writer's family member as needing protection. In 'The Manhunt', instead of the obvious representation of a soldier as strong and powerful, Laura's husband is likened to fine, precious china, "the damaged, porcelain collar-bone". This gives the reader a sense of his fragility following his injuries, with his punctured lung described as delicate "parachute silk". These images show Laura's tenderness for her husband and how she wants to protect him. Similarly, Scannell also chooses the imagery of war for what is really only a minor childhood incident. He refers to the "spears" of the nettles, calling them a "regiment" and, when he has cut them down and they have grown back again, he refers to them as "tall recruits". This battle imagery helps the reader to understand the deeper, metaphorical meaning of his poem; that it is not just about comforting his son from the pain of the nettles, but also about the future pain which he knows he will experience in his life. He knows that "My son would often feel sharp wounds again".

Talk about similarities between the two poems.

Link your points back to the theme of relationships.

Keep making comparisons.

Back up your points with quotes from the poem.

3 Form and Structure

Armitage and Scannell both use a strict rhyme scheme. 'The Manhunt' uses rhyming couplets, with each couplet used to separate out the different injuries the soldier has, including the scar on his face, the broken jaw and his damaged collar-bone. The cheerful and simple rhyme scheme contrasts with the serious subject matter and highlights the complexity of his mental anguish, with the "unexploded mine / buried deep in his mind". The half-rhyme of "mine" and "mind" creates a clear link between the potential sudden violence of an exploding mine and the mental state of the soldier. The simple rhyme scheme of ABAB which is repeated throughout 'Nettles' is also a contrast to the underlying theme of pain and suffering which, in the writer's pessimistic view, his son will have to suffer through his life.

Write about form and structure.

You have to write about the effect these features have too.

Develop your ideas.

Mark Scheme

If I were you, I'd be pretty keen to find out what the examiner expected of me right about now. Oh yes, it'd definitely feature somewhere in my top 20 things to do when bored. Maybe top 50.

Look at What You Have to Do to Get Each Grade

Seriously, it's dead important to know what you have to do to get the grade you're aiming for.

Grade	What you've written
A*	• Explores several interpretations or meanings in detail • Provides carefully chosen and well-integrated quotes to back up ideas • Compares the poems thoughtfully and in detail, using plenty of evidence • Looks closely at how language, form and structure affect the reader with well-chosen examples • Gives detailed and imaginative ideas about themes, attitudes and feelings • Considers the evidence to come up with conclusions about the poem
A	• Gives several interpretations or meanings • Provides well-chosen quotes to support ideas • Compares the poems in detail and provides plenty of evidence • Describes how language, form and structure affect the reader, using examples • Looks at themes, attitudes and feelings in detail, again using plenty of evidence
B	• Thoughtful interpretation of the poems • Supports interpretations with quotes from the text • Provides some well-chosen evidence to support comparisons between the poems • Gives several examples of how language, form and structure affect the reader • Provides some evidence to support ideas about themes, attitudes and feelings
C	• Comments on several aspects of the poem, e.g. mood, language, feelings, and uses quotes to back the comments up • Makes several comparisons between the poems • Explains how language, form and structure affect the reader • Makes valid comments about themes, attitudes or feelings in the poems

You'll also be marked on your spelling, punctuation and grammar and on how you present your work. To get the best marks, your essay should be clearly organised into well-structured paragraphs. It should also be easy to follow and understand.

Sample Question 2

Okey doke, here's another <u>Sample Question</u> for you — it's <u>number two</u> of <u>three</u>, you lucky thing. Have a think about how <u>you'd</u> answer it, then turn over for an <u>example</u> of how you could do it.

Here's Sample Question 2

This is another <u>example</u> of the type of question that might come up in your <u>exam</u>. Remember to <u>read</u> the question <u>carefully</u> and <u>underline key words</u>.

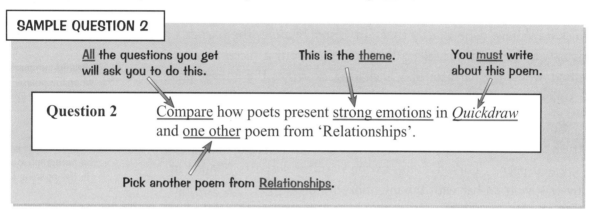

SAMPLE QUESTION 2

<u>All</u> the questions you get will ask you to do this.

This is the <u>theme</u>.

You <u>must</u> write about this poem.

Question 2   <u>Compare</u> how poets present <u>strong emotions</u> in *Quickdraw* and <u>one other</u> poem from 'Relationships'.

Pick another poem from <u>Relationships</u>.

Here's an Example Plan for Sample Question 2

Here's an example of a <u>different way</u> you could plan your answer. Remember, you need to start thinking up <u>comparisons</u> between the poems at the <u>planning stage</u>.

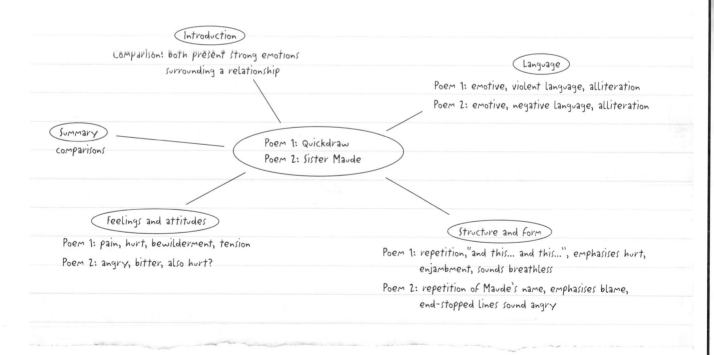

Introduction
Comparison! both present strong emotions surrounding a relationship

Language
Poem 1: emotive, violent language, alliteration
Poem 2: emotive, negative language, alliteration

Summary
comparisons

Poem 1: Quickdraw
Poem 2: Sister Maude

Feelings and attitudes
Poem 1: pain, hurt, bewilderment, tension
Poem 2: angry, bitter, also hurt?

Structure and form
Poem 1: repetition,"and this... and this...", emphasises hurt, enjambment, sounds breathless
Poem 2: repetition of Maude's name, emphasises blame, end-stopped lines sound angry

Try out different types of plans to see what's best for you...

When you're writing answers to <u>practice exam questions</u>, try doing your <u>plan</u> a bit <u>differently</u> each time — that way, you can work out the <u>best way</u> to <u>organise your ideas</u> before the real thing.

How to Answer the Question

Here's an 'A' grade sample answer to the exam question on p.59.

<u>Compare how poets present strong emotions in Quickdraw and one other poem from 'Relationships'.</u>

1 Introduction

Poets often use their work to explore the strong emotions that surround relationships and the writers of 'Sister Maude' and 'Quickdraw' have done exactly that. In 'Sister Maude', the narrator is furious with her sister for telling their parents about a secret love affair she had, whilst the narrator of 'Quickdraw' expresses the intense pain she suffers as a result of her inconsiderate lover's phone calls.

Tell the examiner how the poems relate to the theme.

Briefly summarise what the poems are about in the intro.

2 Language

Both poets use emotive, negative language to express the feelings of their characters. In 'Sister Maude' Rossetti uses the phrase "lurked to spy and peer". "Lurked" suggests the narrator suspects Maude of furtively spying on her with the intention of hurting her. As a result of this, the narrator's desire for revenge is all the more powerful. In order to avenge her sister's spiteful actions, she wishes Maude "no sleep / Either early or late". This suggests she wants Maude to suffer even after she is dead — a particularly extreme and bitter sentiment. Like Rossetti, Duffy also uses some quite violent imagery to convey her narrator's pain. She uses words associated with weaponry and conflict to describe how her lover's words affect her: "your voice a pellet". The two lovers are portrayed as being part of a Wild West gunfight, involved in a cruel game of quickdraw that the narrator is hopelessly losing: "I reel. / Down on my knees". Both poets use alliteration to emphasise the emotions in their poems. Rossetti, for example, repeats the hard 'C' sound in the phrase, "Cold he lies, as cold as stone, / With his clotted curls...". The harshness of the sound conveys the narrator's chilling anger over her lover's death. In the same way, Duffy uses the alliterative "trigger of my tongue" to emphasise the cruelty in the game her characters are playing.

Make it clear what the paragraph's about in the opening line.

Remember to keep making comparisons.

Use short quotes to back up your points.

Use technical terms where possible.

3 Form and Structure

Both poets use structural devices to express strong emotions. The repetition of her sister's name emphasises that it is Maude the narrator holds responsible, and Maude whom she is furious with. By also repeating the word "sister", the reader feels the strength of her bitterness; this is supposed to be a happy, loving, family relationship, which makes Maude's betrayal greater and more shocking. Duffy also uses repetition to emphasise her narrator's anguish. In the final line the lover's kisses are made to seem like bullets shot from a gun, wounding the narrator with the phrase, "Take this... / and this... and

Remember to stay focused on the question's theme.

How to Answer the Question

this... and this...". Rossetti's use of end-stopped lines stresses the poem's angry rhythm and makes her narrator sound like she is spitting out her words. Duffy on the other hand uses enjambment, splitting the lines irregularly to add to the poem's tension. As a result her narrator sounds breathless and uncertain of what will happen next. Some of the split lines are indented, adding emphasis to their words: "You've wounded me" and "through the heart" provide a neat summary for the key feelings of intense pain in this poem.

Comment on the effect of poetic devices.

Feelings and Attitudes

In both poems, the narrator is portrayed as the victim; each speaker has been hurt as a result of the actions of a loved one. 'Quickdraw' however has none of the righteous and indignant anger of 'Sister Maude'; instead the narrator seems resigned to her fate: "I reel". While Rossetti's character seems to want to cut all ties with her sister, the speaker in 'Quickdraw' still fumbles desperately for the phone each time her lover rings, willing to accept the pain it will cause. Both poems also show that relationships can sometimes have a dark and unpleasant side. The narrator of 'Sister Maude' appears filled with hatred for her sibling: "sister Maude shall get no sleep". This may be because she once loved and trusted her sister so completely that the pain from her betrayal is worse than it would otherwise have been. 'Quickdraw' illustrates that romantic relationships are not always about love and tenderness either. Here, the two lovers are caught up in a cruel competition, each trying to inflict the greater emotional wounds on the other person.

Talk about differences as well as similarities.

Give a personal response.

4

Conclusion

The narrators' strong emotions are clearly and powerfully presented in both 'Sister Maude' and 'Quickdraw'. Although the form of the two poems is quite different, Rossetti and Duffy both use negative and sometimes violent language to convey their characters' feelings. The narrators of both poems have been hurt by someone they love and trust. In 'Sister Maude', this pain translates into bitterness and rage; in 'Quickdraw', it leads to unhappiness and bewilderment. Since many of us will have experienced similar emotions in our own relationships at one time or another, we can easily empathise with the suffering of both individuals.

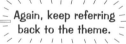

Again, keep referring back to the theme.

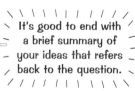

It's good to end with a brief summary of your ideas that refers back to the question.

5

Section Five — The Poetry Exam

Sample Question 3

Most of the questions you get in the exam will be pretty <u>similar</u>. One or two might <u>look</u> a bit different, but they <u>shouldn't</u> cause you any <u>major problems</u> — just follow the <u>advice</u> on this page.

Here's Sample Question 3

Some questions are <u>worded</u> a bit <u>differently</u> — don't let them catch you out. Here's an <u>example</u>:

SAMPLE QUESTION 3

Be <u>careful</u> with this question — it <u>isn't</u> asking you for a <u>rant</u> about how much you hate these poems. The <u>mark scheme</u> is the <u>same</u> as for the other questions — you still need to comment on <u>language</u>, <u>form</u> and <u>structure</u>.

Question 3	Different people prefer different poems. Write about whether you enjoyed the poem *The Farmer's Bride* and <u>compare</u> it to <u>one</u> other poem from 'Relationships' which you either like or dislike. Remember to comment on <u>how the poems are written</u>.

You're still being asked to <u>compare</u> the two poems.

It's <u>not enough</u> just to say which bits you like or dislike.

Here's an Example Plan for Sample Question 3

Here's <u>another way</u> you could plan your answer. The table helps you sort out <u>which quotes</u> you want to use to <u>support each of the points</u> you make.

Intro
Poem 1: The Farmer's Bride, Poem 2: Harmonium
Response: both poems effective at presenting characters in difficult situations

	Poem 1	Poem 2
Form: both narrative poems, different approach	rhyming couplets: "swift as he / ... young larch tree"	free verse, occasional rhyme for emphasis, "freight", "weight"
Different types of lang: Poem 1 — nature, hunting Poem 2 — personification	"frightened fay", "shy as a leveret", "like a mouse", "We chased her"	"hummed harmonics", "yellowed... fingernails", "lost its tongue"
Wider Issues: both create sympathy for central characters	"I've hardly heard her speak at all"	"some shallow or sorry phrase or word"

Preference
FB — clever use of extended metaphor
Harmonium most effective — poignant last line, realism

Always write about language, form and structure...

<u>Don't panic</u> if something a bit odd like this comes up in the exam. It's really asking you to do the <u>same</u> as you would in <u>any other question</u> — so just <u>write your answer</u> in the <u>same way</u>.

THIS IS A FLAP.
FOLD THIS PAGE OUT.

How to Answer the Question

connotations. She also presents the tension between her characters carefully, with telling images of the hunter and the hunted. The bride is depicted as a helpless prey animal — "like a hare", "like a mouse", "Shy as a leveret" — whilst the husband is cast in the role of the predator: "We chased her" and "We caught her". By describing the young farmer's wife in this way, we are given a sense of her vulnerability, as well as her skittishness and almost childlike fear of her husband. While Mew compares the farmer's wife to a wild animal, Armitage brings his harmonium to life using personification. He talks about the "yellowed... fingernails of its keys" and the note that had "lost its tongue". Not only does it help us to picture the ageing instrument, it also helps us to make the metaphorical link between the harmonium and the poet's father with his yellowed "smoker's fingers and dottled thumbs". This link is important; the organ which had "hummed harmonics... / for a hundred years" is now "worn" and useless, unable to properly carry out its function. The poet's father also sees himself as past his usefulness as he ponders his own coffin being carried from the church in a similar manner to the harmonium.

Develop your ideas for more marks.

Make lots of links between the poems.

Both poets manage to elicit real sympathy from the reader for their central characters. It is easy to feel sorry for the nervous young farmer's wife who "runned away" only to be brought back under lock and "key", but Mew also gives us a real sense of her husband's confusion and bewilderment over the situation. While his wife is willing to talk to the "birds and rabbits", the farmer has "hardly heard her speak at all", something he seems unable to explain or comprehend. In 'Harmonium', Armitage effectively presents the awkwardness that children feel when talking about death with their parents, leaving an uncomfortable silence between them, "too starved of breath to make itself heard". We are left with the impression that the embarrassed narrator wishes he could say more to comfort his father and express his true feelings on the subject — instead of "some shallow or sorry phrase or word" — but clearly feels unable to. It is something many of us may be able to relate to, as is the father's fear (covered by his attempt at humour) of himself someday becoming old and obsolete.

The question is about why you like or dislike the poem — so say what it does or doesn't do well.

Your writing will flow better if your quotes are embedded into your sentences.

You get marks for a personal response.

'The Farmer's Bride' and 'Harmonium' are both extremely successful at telling their stories, engaging the reader and, above all, evoking empathy. 'The Farmer's Bride' makes effective use of an extended hunting metaphor but it is 'Harmonium' that really stands out, perhaps because it talks about a situation we can all easily recognise. It is a subtle but thought-provoking narrative, which concludes with a poignant silence.

Finish with a strong conclusion that refers back to the question.

How to Answer the Question

Here's an 'A' grade sample answer to the exam question on p.62.

<u>Different people prefer different poems. Write about whether you enjoyed the poem The Farmer's Bride and compare it to one other poem from 'Relationships' which you either like or dislike. Remember to comment on how the poems are written.</u>

Introduction ①

Both 'The Farmer's Bride' and 'Harmonium' are extremely effective narrative poems, which tell believable stories and create realistic images of the relationships they are describing. The two poets present sympathetic and convincing characters who are finding it hard to cope in difficult situations. In 'The Farmer's Bride', the narrator of the poem is a farmer whose bride is scared of him; before they married she used to "smile", but she is now "More like a little frightened fay". He is confused, unable to understand why every time he approaches her, she recoils: "'Not near, not near!' Her eyes beseech". Similarly, the reader is led to feel sympathy for the narrator of 'Harmonium', who struggles to find the words when it comes to talking about death. Despite his father's attempts at humour on the subject, he is able only to "mouth in reply" a weak and unsatisfactory response to the joke.

Form ②

Part of Harmonium's realism comes from its form. It is written in free verse, with no rhyme scheme or metre. This helps Armitage to tell the story in a thoughtful and natural way, moving skilfully from the description of the old organ to that of the old man and his contemplation of death, finally ending with the poet's awkwardness at his father's words. He uses occasional rhyme to add emphasis to key lines; for example, the blunt sounding "freight" and "weight" add a sense of certainty to his father's death. Form is also important in 'The Farmer's Bride', although Charlotte Mew uses a more regular rhyme scheme for her poem. This includes a number of rhyming couplets and, in later stanzas, groups of three (and at one point four) rhyming lines when the farmer is describing how physically attractive he finds his young wife: "Straight and slight as a young larch tree". These add pace to the poem, as well as giving a sense of the farmer's increasing tension, and reflect his inability to control his desire for her any longer. This leaves the reader wondering whether the farmer will be able to control himself or whether he will take her by force.

Mew cleverly sets the scene for the hunting metaphors with her references to farming and nature. We can easily visualise the fields and downs at "harvest-time", with the brown oaks and "low grey sky" of winter, but these usually peaceful images have more sinister

Start comparing the poems as early in your answer as possible.

Use sophisticated vocabulary.

It's helpful to plan what quotes you want to use.

Using technical terms correctly will get you marks.

It's good to have examples for form and structure too.

Write about <u>how</u> features like form and language create an effect.

The Controlled Assessment

If you're following <u>Route B</u> of the AQA English Literature course, you'll have to do a <u>controlled assessment</u> task for <u>Unit 5: Exploring Poetry</u>. That's what this page is about.

This is How Unit 5 Works

1) Your teacher will set you a question on some <u>poetry</u>. They might decide to use poems from the poetry <u>Anthology</u> that's covered in this book.

2) The question will ask you to compare <u>contemporary poems</u> (like those in Section 2) with ones from the <u>Literary Heritage</u> (Section 1).

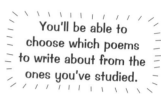

You'll be able to choose which poems to write about from the ones you've studied.

3) You might have to <u>listen to</u> or <u>watch</u> performances of the poems and write about them in your answer.

4) You're expected to write around <u>2000 words</u>. Your answer is worth <u>25%</u> of your <u>final GCSE grade</u>.

You're Allowed to Plan Your Answer First

1) You'll be able to spend time in class <u>planning</u> and <u>preparing</u> for this essay.

2) During this time, you'll be allowed to look at <u>books</u> and the <u>Internet</u> and <u>ask</u> your teacher <u>questions</u>. You must make a <u>note</u> of anything you use to help you (e.g. a website) in a bibliography.

3) You can write a <u>rough draft</u> if you want, but you <u>won't</u> be able to have it with you while you're writing up your answer. You can take in <u>brief notes</u> though.

You'll Have Up to Four Hours to Write Up Your Answer

1) You can write up your answer in your classroom over a few lessons, but you'll be under <u>exam conditions</u>.

For Sam's control assessment he had to demonstrate skilful changing of channels.

2) You'll be given unmarked <u>copies</u> of the poems to help you.

3) You can write up your essay <u>by hand</u>, or type it up on a <u>computer</u>.

> You'll be allowed a <u>dictionary</u> or to use your <u>spell-check</u>, but if you do have a computer you <u>won't</u> be able to get on the <u>Internet</u>.

4) Your work will be <u>collected in</u> at the end of every session. When you've finished, your teacher will collect in <u>everything</u> you've written — including any drafts you did earlier on.

You'll write up the task under exam conditions...

So, your teacher will set you a <u>question</u> on some poems you've studied. You'll have <u>time</u> to <u>prepare</u> your answer, but you're expected to <u>write it up</u> in a maximum of <u>four</u> supervised hours.

The Controlled Assessment

I expect you'd find it helpful to know what <u>kind of questions</u> you're going to get asked, how best to <u>approach</u> them and what you'll be <u>marked</u> on. So I've done a nice page about it for you.

You'll Be Marked on Three Main Things

<u>Whatever</u> question you get, you'll get marks for doing these <u>three</u> things.

Keep them in mind when you're <u>planning</u> and <u>writing</u> your answer.

① Giving your own <u>thoughts</u> and <u>opinions</u> on the poems and supporting the points you make with <u>quotes</u> from the text.

② <u>Explaining</u> features like <u>form</u>, <u>structure</u> and <u>language</u>.

③ Describing the <u>similarities</u> and <u>differences</u> between poems.

This means you should always <u>compare</u> the poems you're writing about.

Here Are Some Example Questions

EXAMPLE QUESTION 1

Explore the ways different types of relationships are presented in the texts you have studied.

EXAMPLE QUESTION 2

Explore how poets use structure and form to create an effect in a range of contemporary and Literary Heritage poems.

1) You can <u>choose</u> which poems you write about, but you <u>must</u> include <u>at least</u> <u>one contemporary</u> and <u>one Literary Heritage</u> poem. The number of poems you write about is <u>up to you</u>, but make sure you have <u>plenty to say</u> about each one.

2) Even though the question doesn't specifically ask you to <u>compare</u> the poems, that's what you <u>have to do</u> to get good marks.

Think About How You're Going to Tackle the Question

The question you get might be quite <u>general</u>, so you're going to have to think about the <u>best way</u> to approach it. You might find it <u>helpful</u> to start off with a <u>basic plan</u> like the one below.

- Choose poems which relate to the <u>theme</u> of the question.
- Look at the <u>language</u> — what effect does it create? <u>How</u> does it do this?
- Look at the <u>form and structure</u> — what effect do they create? <u>How</u> do they do this?
- What are the <u>feelings and attitudes</u> in the poems?

How do the poems <u>compare</u> with each other?

Prepare your answer carefully...

The question is usually set by your teacher, but you'll always be <u>marked</u> in the <u>same way</u>. Always write about <u>language</u>, <u>form</u> and <u>structure</u>, as well as the <u>feelings and attitudes</u> in the poems.

The Controlled Assessment

A <u>good plan</u> will help you organise your thoughts and write a <u>clear</u>, <u>well-structured</u> essay — which means lots of <u>lovely marks</u>. And the good news is, you'll have <u>plenty of time</u> to prepare one.

Choose Your Poems **and** Map Out Ideas

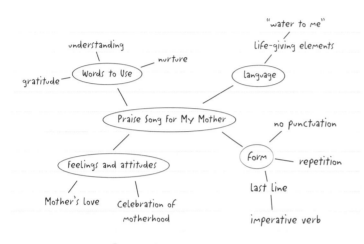

1) Let's say that for <u>Example Question 1</u> on page 65, you decide to write about <u>Praise Song For My Mother</u>.

2) You might want to <u>map out</u> your <u>ideas</u> like on the left, so you can decide what to include in your detailed <u>plan</u>.

3) It's a good idea to do this for <u>all</u> your poems and make <u>links</u> between them.

4) Write down some <u>key quotes</u> you want to include in your essay too.

Write a Detailed Plan

Here's an <u>example plan</u> for Question 1 on the last page. You can make it fairly <u>detailed</u>, as you've got enough time.

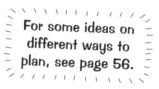

For some ideas on different ways to plan, see page 56.

Introduction

What essay is about
Negative poems: Sister Maude, In Paris with You
Positive poems: Praise Song for My Mother, The Manhunt

Feelings and Attitudes
- Sister Maude — anger at betrayal
- In Paris — bitterness at rejection
- Praise Song — celebration of mother's love
- The Manhunt — wife's protective love towards injured husband

Language
- Sister Maude — emotive — "lurked"
- In Paris — emotive — "wounded"
- Praise Song — life-giving elements (sun, water, food)
- The Manhunt — link between physical injuries + mental state — "mine" / "mind" half rhyme

Form and Structure
- Sister Maude — short lines, alternating rhyme = tight-lipped fury
- In Paris — half rhymes = unsatisfactory, like current relationship
- Praise Song — rhythm changes, no punctuation, final line
- The Manhunt — rhyming couplets contrast cheerful rhyme scheme and serious subject matter

Conclusion
- Praise Song and Manhunt show intense and positive relationships, Sister Maude and In Paris present bitter feelings

Plan what you're going to write about before you start...

Use your preparation time <u>wisely</u> to come up with a <u>good plan</u> for your essay. You won't be allowed it with you when you're writing up, but you can have a <u>few notes</u> to jog your memory.

The Controlled Assessment

Here are some grade 'A' paragraphs from a sample answer to Example Question 1 on page 65.

Here's a Sample Introduction

Write an introduction that makes it clear you've understood the question, like this one:

> Poetic form is often used to express the strong and complex emotions experienced in relationships. These can be either positive, fulfilling relationships where the speaker is comfortable or even ecstatic about their feelings or they can be completely the opposite, with expressions of confusion, bitterness, guilt or even utter hatred. Poems which present the more pleasant parts of a relationship include 'Praise Song For My Mother' and 'The Manhunt', whilst 'Sister Maude' and 'In Paris with You' explore significantly more unpleasant sentiments.

← Tell the reader the names of the poems you're going to discuss.

Here are Some Sample Paragraphs

You've got 2000 words to really explore the poems in depth. You don't have to write about every little bit of the poems — focus on writing about a few key elements in detail.

> Both 'Sister Maude' and 'In Paris With You' are written in the voice of a character who is particularly bitter at a betrayal by someone close to them. In 'Sister Maude', the narrator blames Maude for telling their parents about a secret relationship she was in: "Who told my father of my dear? / Oh who but Maude". By using rhetorical questions at the beginning she makes it quite clear whose fault it is that they found out. In addition, her constant repetition of "Maude" reiterates that it is because of her sister's interference that her lover is now a "corpse". The repetition of the word "Sister" emphasises this hatred; this should be a relationship of mutual support, but here it has led to distrust and malice. The narrator accuses Maude, "Who lurked to spy and peer"; the use of the word "lurked" suggests that Maude's actions were furtive and that she had every intention of betraying her sister.
>
> Similar use of a rhetorical question and repetition is found in 'In Paris With You'...

← Make it clear what each paragraph's about in the first line.

← Aim to develop your ideas.

← Analyse the language closely.

← Remember to compare the poems.

It's important to give your own opinions on the poems. Make your interpretations sound more convincing by giving plenty of evidence to support your argument — this means using lots of quotes.

> 'The Manhunt' uses this very intimate relationship between husband and wife to leave the reader with a message which is more universal. Despite presenting this as a close, loving relationship, the pain and suffering surrounding it is expressed in the "unexploded mine / buried deep in his mind". The half-rhyme link between the potential danger of the mine, which could explode suddenly at any time, and the soldier's unstable mental state of mind, makes the reader think carefully about the effects of war on individuals. Rather than writing about many soldiers, Armitage has chosen to write in detail about the effects of conflict on this one soldier and his wife. He seems to want the reader to consider the less public effects of conflicts and focus on the repercussions military warfare has on the families and relationships of those involved.

← Keep focused on the theme of the question.

← Look at the poem's wider messages.

← Give your own personal interpretations.

How to Write an A* Answer

It's what you've all been waiting for: absolutely <u>everything</u> you need to know to write an <u>utterly fantastic</u>, knock-the-examiner's-socks-off, quite-frankly-blummin'-amazing <u>A* answer</u>. Phew. Better have a cuppa first.

Know Your Texts In Depth

1) Make sure you know the poems <u>really well</u> — you need to be able to write about them <u>in detail</u>.

2) <u>Don't</u> just re-tell the <u>story</u> of the poem in your essay though — and <u>don't</u> try to write down absolutely <u>everything</u> you know about it.

3) Instead, <u>carefully</u> select <u>key bits</u> of the text and <u>focus</u> on writing about them <u>in depth</u>.

Look Closely at Language

To get <u>top marks</u>, you need to pay <u>close attention</u> to the <u>language</u> used in the poems.

Use technical terms wherever you can.

Always develop your ideas.

> In 'Nettles', Scannell uses military vocabulary to describe the plants and their stinging barbs. Words such as "green spears", "regiment", "fierce parade" and "tall recruits" all create a vivid image of soldiers engaged in battle in the mind of the reader. The poet's use of the adjective "fierce" enhances the personification of these plants as being aggressive and violent, giving a sense of human spite to their infliction of wounds and pain. By using such brutal imagery, Scannell seems to suggest that, in life, pain is often inflicted on purpose by others; an unpleasant thought for a father to contemplate.

Analyse the effects of key words.

Use synonyms to help explain the poet's language.

Give Alternative Interpretations

1) You need to show you're aware that poems can be <u>interpreted</u> in <u>more than one</u> way.

2) If the poem's a bit <u>ambiguous</u>, or you think that a particular line or phrase could have several <u>different meanings</u>, then <u>say so</u>.

> In 'Brothers' we are never actually told whether the younger child is one of the brothers of the title. Although a more obvious reading is that this child is the younger brother, there is some evidence to suggest that "me and Paul" are the brothers and that the child they are "Saddled" with is perhaps a sister. Supporting this reading is their contempt at her attempts to talk about football — "spouting six-year-old views on Rotherham United" — and the "ridiculous tank-top", which is often seen as more an item of girls' clothing.

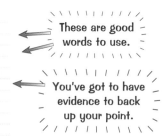

These are good words to use.

You've got to have evidence to back up your point.

3) Don't be afraid to be <u>original</u> with your ideas — you get <u>marks</u> for a <u>personal response</u>. Just make sure you can back up your arguments with <u>plenty of evidence</u> from the poem.

Give some imaginative ideas...

You could <u>gain</u> marks for saying something a bit <u>different</u>, but you <u>must</u> be able to <u>support</u> your theories with <u>quotes</u> — otherwise you'll look like you don't know what you're <u>talking about</u>.

How to Write an A* Answer

Even if your teachers aren't predicting you an A*, it's still worth looking at these pages to get a few ideas on how you could improve your work. This quoting lark for example — everyone should have a glance at that.

Always Support Your Ideas with Details from the Text

This might seem like a fairly basic point — but if you don't back up your ideas with quotes or references from the text, then you're not going to get top marks. Here are some quoting top tips:

1) Choose your quotes carefully — they have to be relevant to the point you're making.

✓ ...According to the narrator, Maude "lurked to spy and peer". This suggests intentional duplicity and dishonesty...

✗ Barrett Browning says that she will love her husband "to the depth and breadth and height / [Her] soul can reach, when feeling out of sight / For the ends of Being and ideal Grace".

This bit's not needed.

2) Don't quote large chunks of text — it's not necessary and it wastes time.

3) Don't reel off long lists of quotes without explaining them. Remember, quotes are there as evidence to support your argument.

✗ Larkin lists the conventional attributes that others would wish upon a newborn baby: "being beautiful", "innocence and love". He then goes on to say what characteristics he'd wish for the girl: "ordinary", "an average of talents", "not good-looking".

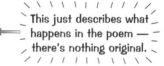
This just describes what happens in the poem — there's nothing original.

✓ Larkin's tone changes completely and becomes one of harsh realism as he goes on to say what characteristics he would wish upon the girl. Words such as "ordinary" and "average" definitively capture his belief that "being beautiful" is not what is needed for a child to have a happy future.

This is much better.

Show Some Wider Knowledge

1) Do some research on the poets. Although you don't have to include context, it'll still look pretty impressive.

2) Don't go overboard though — your facts might be interesting, but you have to show they're relevant to your answer. It's best to keep your comments fairly short.

Grace Nichols draws on her Caribbean upbringing when she uses the vivid imagery of the foods from her childhood to ignite the reader's senses: we can envisage the wonderful, vibrant colours of "the fish's red gill" and imagine the smell of the traditional, banana-like fruit, "fried plantain".

By comparing the religiously symbolic, world-renowned Ganges with his local home-town River Humber, Marvell makes his audience aware of the irony in his words. When telling his "mistress" how much time he wishes he could have with her, he is actually demonstrating to her how ridiculous her "coyness" is.

Wider knowledge — sounds dangerous to me...

Quotes. Can't live with 'em, can't live without 'em as I believe the saying goes. Or a saying anyway. Think carefully about which ones to use and where, that's my advice. Sorted.

How to Write an A* Answer

It's not just <u>what</u> you write that gets you an A* grade, it's <u>how</u> you write it.
Show some <u>finesse</u> with a <u>tip top vocabulary</u> and a lovely <u>flowing</u> writing <u>style</u>.

Use Sophisticated Language

1) To put it simply, your writing has to sound <u>sophisticated</u> and <u>stylish</u>.
2) It should be <u>concise</u> and <u>accurate</u>, with no <u>vague words</u> or <u>waffle</u>.
3) It should also show off an <u>impressive range</u> of <u>vocabulary</u>.
4) Make sure it's <u>appropriate</u> though — <u>don't</u> use words if you don't know what they really <u>mean</u>.

Style and sophistication are Eddie's watchwords.

Not very sophisticated. → Forster's narrator seems sad that he left his sibling behind...

The narrator's sense of guilt becomes increasingly obvious... ← This sounds much better.

This is too vague. → Shakespeare uses a lot of imagery...

Shakespeare uses a wide range of imagery... ← Use more specific language.

Don't keep using the same word to describe something. → The narrator of 'In Paris With You' is clearly angry about the way his last relationship ended. He feels angry at being rejected. This anger even seems to extend towards his new partner.

The narrator of 'In Paris With You' is clearly angry about the way his last relationship ended. He feels pain and bitterness about being "bamboozled". This hatred even seems to extend towards his new partner. ← Vary how you say things — it's far more interesting.

Use Technical Terms Where Possible

At A* level, you need to use the <u>correct technical terms</u> when you're talking about poetry. There's a handy <u>glossary</u> at the back of this guide that explains a lot of these terms for you.

<u>Don't write:</u>	<u>Write:</u>
✗ Mew uses weird words...	✓ Mew uses dialect to...
✗ The sentences run on from one line to the next...	✓ The poet uses enjambment to...
✗ The poet uses touchy-feely words.	✓ The poet uses emotive language...

Think carefully about your choice of words...

You've got to sound like you <u>really know</u> what you're talking about — and the words you use to do it will make a <u>big difference</u>. This kind of writing gets <u>a lot easier</u> with <u>practice</u> — so practise.

How to Write an A* Answer

There's <u>more</u> to writing an <u>A* answer</u> than you thought, eh? Still, we're <u>nearly done</u>.
This last page is a <u>real winner</u>, I'm sure you'll agree, so let's get cracking.

Vary Your Sentence Structures

It's important to keep your reader <u>interested</u> in what you're saying. One way to do
that is to vary the <u>style</u> and <u>length</u> of your sentences. Look at these <u>examples</u>:

This is <u>boring</u> — it's dull and <u>repetitive</u>...

> He seems to have a sense of humour. He says that his mistress is "coy".
> This shows that he thinks she is shy, but possibly a little bit sly. This seems unexpected
> in a lover. He says his lust for her is "vegetable". What he means by this is...

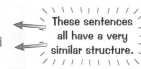
These sentences all have a very similar structure.

This is <u>varied</u> and much more <u>interesting</u>...

Use simple sentences to introduce a point, then more complex ones to expand on it.

> Andrew Marvell betrays a sense of humour in 'To His Coy
> Mistress', even in the poem's title. The use of the word "coy" implies a
> put-upon shyness, perhaps even a certain slyness, that seems unexpected
> in a lover. He continues to poke gentle fun at the situation, referring to
> his lust for her as "vegetable": a basic, earthy, unromantic desire.

Use a variety of punctuation, including colons (:) and semi-colons (;), when appropriate.

Your Writing Should Flow Around Your Quotes

To get an A*, your writing needs to <u>flow</u> beautifully.
This means working your quotes seamlessly into your sentences.

<u>For example</u>, instead of writing this...

> Armitage describes the harmonium as old and useless:
> "holes were worn in both the treadles", "notes had lost
> its tongue", "yellowed...fingernails of its keys".

This sounds a bit awkward.

...it's much <u>better</u> to write this:

> With holes "worn in both the treadles" and a note that "had lost
> its tongue", Armitage's harmonium is now old and past its best.

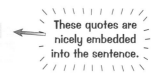
These quotes are nicely embedded into the sentence.

"Your writing should flow around your quotes like a river flows around stones."
CGP, 2010

Proof-Read Your Work

1)   To get top marks, you need to avoid errors in <u>spelling</u>, <u>punctuation</u> and <u>grammar</u>.

2)   Once you've finished your work, spend time <u>checking</u> it over and <u>correcting</u> any <u>mistakes</u>.

3)   In the <u>exam</u>, leave yourself <u>five minutes</u> to read through your answer at the end.
     Put a <u>neat line</u> through any mistakes and write the correction <u>above</u>.

4)   In your <u>controlled assessment</u>, you're allowed more time and access to a dictionary or spell-check.
     This means your work will be marked much more <u>strictly</u> — so check it <u>carefully</u>.

Leave time to prof-reed yuor work...

It might sound basic, but you seriously do need to <u>check your work</u> once you've finished. It's easy
to make <u>silly mistakes</u> even if you're being really careful — and silly mistakes <u>don't look impressive</u>.

Glossary

adjective	A word that <u>describes</u> something, e.g. "big", "fast", "annoying".
alliteration	Where words that are close together <u>start</u> with the <u>same letter</u>. It's often used in poetry to give a nice pattern to a phrase. E.g. "<u>h</u>ummed <u>h</u>armonics".
ambiguity	Where a word or phrase has <u>two or more</u> possible <u>meanings</u>.
assonance	When words share the same <u>vowel sound</u> but the consonants are different. E.g. "th<u>u</u>mb / l<u>u</u>ng".
autobiographical	Describing something that happened in the <u>poet's life</u>.
ballad	A form of <u>poetry</u> that tells a <u>story</u> and often sounds quite <u>musical</u>.
blank verse	Poetry written in iambic pentameter that <u>doesn't rhyme</u>, but has a regular <u>rhythm</u>.
caesura	A <u>pause</u> in a line. E.g. Around the full stop in "I'm a hostage. I'm marooned."
colloquial	Sounding like everyday <u>spoken</u> language, e.g. "the usual stuff".
consonance	When words have the <u>same</u> consonant sounds but <u>different</u> vowel sounds, e.g. "hurt", "heart".
consonants	All the letters in the alphabet that <u>aren't vowels</u>.
contrast	When two things are described in a way which emphasises <u>how different</u> they are. E.g. A poet might contrast two different places or two different people.
dialect	A <u>variation</u> of a <u>language</u>. People from different places might use different words or sentence constructions, e.g. the non-standard grammar in "She runned away".
emotive	Something that makes you <u>feel</u> a particular <u>emotion</u>.
empathy	When someone feels like they <u>understand</u> what someone else is experiencing and how they <u>feel</u> about it.
end-stopping	Finishing a line of poetry with the <u>end</u> of a <u>phrase or sentence</u>.
enjambment	When a sentence runs over from <u>one line</u> or <u>stanza</u> to the <u>next</u>.
first person	When someone writes about themselves, or a group which includes them, using words like "<u>I</u>", "<u>my</u>" and "<u>me</u>".
form	The <u>type</u> of poem, e.g. a sonnet or a ballad, and its <u>features</u>, like number of lines, rhyme, rhythm and metre.
free verse	Poetry that <u>doesn't rhyme</u> and has <u>no regular rhythm</u>.
iambic pentameter	Poetry with a <u>metre</u> of <u>ten syllables</u> — five of them stressed, and five unstressed. The <u>stress</u> falls on <u>every second syllable</u>, e.g. "My <u>soul</u> can <u>reach</u> when <u>feeling out</u> of <u>sight</u>".
iambic tetrameter	Like iambic pentameter but with a metre of <u>eight</u> syllables — four stressed and four unstressed. E.g. "She <u>does</u> the <u>work</u> about the <u>house</u>."
imagery	Language that creates a <u>picture in your mind</u>. It includes <u>metaphors</u> and <u>similes</u>.
internal rhyme	When a word in the <u>middle</u> of a line rhymes with the <u>last</u> word of the line. E.g. "Next time, you speak after the <u>tone</u>. I twirl the <u>phone</u>".
irony	When <u>words</u> are used in a <u>sarcastic</u> or <u>comic</u> way to <u>imply the opposite</u> of what they normally mean. It can also mean when there is a big difference between <u>what people expect</u> and <u>what actually happens</u>.
language	The <u>choice of words</u> used. Different kinds of language have <u>different effects</u>.

Glossary

layout	The way a piece of poetry is visually <u>presented</u> to the reader, e.g. line length, whether the poem is broken up into different stanzas, whether lines create some kind of visual pattern.
metaphor	A way of describing something by saying that it <u>is something else</u>, to create a vivid image. E.g. "the parachute silk of his punctured lung".
metre	The arrangement of syllables to create <u>rhythm</u> in a line of poetry.
monologue	<u>One person</u> speaking for a long period of time.
mood	The <u>feel</u> or <u>atmosphere</u> of a poem, e.g. humorous, threatening, eerie.
narrative	Writing that tells a <u>story</u>, e.g. the poem 'Brothers'.
narrator	The <u>voice</u> speaking the words that you're reading. E.g. A poem could be written from the point of view of a young child, which means the young child is the poem's narrator.
oxymoron	A phrase which appears to <u>contradict</u> itself, because the words have meanings that <u>don't</u> seem to <u>fit together</u>, e.g. "comeliest corpse".
persona	A <u>fictional character</u> or <u>identity</u> adopted by a poet. Poets often create a persona so they can describe things from a different person's <u>point of view</u>, e.g. a male poet might use a female persona.
personification	A special kind of metaphor where you write about something as if it's a <u>person</u> with <u>thoughts</u> and <u>feelings</u>. E.g. "Love alters not with his brief hours and weeks".
rhyme scheme	A <u>pattern</u> of rhyming words in a poem, e.g. in 'Nettles', the 1st line rhymes with the 3rd, and the 2nd rhymes with the 4th.
rhyming couplet	A <u>pair of rhyming lines</u> that are next to each other, e.g. the last two lines of 'Hour'.
rhythm	A <u>pattern of sounds</u> created by the arrangement of <u>stressed</u> and <u>unstressed</u> syllables.
sibilance	Repetition of '<u>s</u>' and '<u>sh</u>' sounds.
simile	A way of describing something by <u>comparing</u> it to something else, usually by using the words "like" or "as", e.g. "flying like a hare".
sonnet	A form of poem with <u>fourteen lines</u>, and usually following a <u>clear rhyme pattern</u>. There are different types of sonnets. They're often about <u>love</u>.
stanza	A <u>group of lines</u> in a poem. Stanzas can also be called <u>verses</u>.
structure	The <u>order</u> and <u>arrangement</u> of ideas and events in a piece of writing, e.g. how the poem begins, develops and ends.
syllable	A single <u>unit of sound</u> within a word. E.g. "All" has one syllable, "always" has two and "establishmentarianism" has nine.
symbolism	When an object <u>stands for something else</u>. E.g. A candle might be a symbol of hope, or a dying flower could symbolise the end of a relationship.
theme	An <u>idea</u> or <u>topic</u> that's important in a piece of writing. E.g. A poem could be based on the theme of friendship.
tone	The <u>mood</u> or <u>feelings</u> suggested by the way the narrator <u>writes</u>, e.g. confident, thoughtful.
voice	The <u>personality</u> narrating the poem. Poems are usually written either using the poet's voice, as if they're speaking to you <u>directly</u>, or the voice of a <u>character</u>.
vowels	The letters "a", "e", "i", "o" and "u".

<u>*Index*</u>

Index

Acknowledgements

The Publisher would like to thank:

For poems:
Simon Armitage: 'Harmonium' — Copyright © Simon Armitage
Simon Armitage: 'The Manhunt' — Reproduced with the permission of Pomona on behalf of Simon Armitage, 2008
Carol Ann Duffy: 'Hour' — From *Rapture* (Picador, 2005) reproduced with the permission of Picador, an imprint of Pan Macmillan, London. Copyright © Carol Ann Duffy 2005
Carol Ann Duffy: 'Quickdraw' — From *Rapture* (Picador, 2005) reproduced with the permission of Picador, an imprint of Pan Macmillan, London. Copyright © Carol Ann Duffy 2005
James Fenton: 'In Paris With You' — Reprinted by permission of United Agents on behalf of James Fenton
Andrew Forster: 'Brothers' — From *Fear of Thunder*, Flambard Press
Mimi Khalvati: 'Ghazal' — From *The Meanest Flower*, Carcanet Press Ltd (26 Jul 2007)
Philip Larkin: 'Born Yesterday' — From *The Less Deceived*, the Marvell Press, 1955, ISBN 978-0900533068
Grace Nichols: 'Praise Song For My Mother' — Reproduced with permission of Curtis Brown Group Ltd, London on behalf of Grace Nichols Copyright © Grace Nichols 1984
Vernon Scannell: 'Nettles' — From *New and Collected Poems* reproduced with the permission of Macmillan Children's Books, London, UK

For photographs:
Simon Armitage, Carol Ann Duffy, James Fenton, Grace Nichols — Rex Features
Elizabeth Barrett Browning, Andrew Marvell, Christina Rossetti, William Shakespeare — Mary Evans Picture Library
Andrew Forster — Andrew Forster/Flambard Press
Mimi Khalvati — Mimi Khalvati/Carcanet Press Ltd
Philip Larkin — Photograph by Godfrey Argent, Camera Press London
Charlotte Mew — Charlotte Mew/Carcanet Press Ltd